The Keystone

by

Anita J. Moore

DORRANCE PUBLISHING CO., INC.
PITTSBURGH, PENNSYLVANIA 15222

All Rights Reserved
Copyright © 2004 by Anita J. Moore
No part of this book may be reproduced or transmitted
in any form or by any means, electronic or mechanical,
including photocopying, recording, or by any information
storage and retrieval system without permission in
writing from the publisher.

ISBN # 0-8059-6351-0
Printed in the United States of America

First Printing

For information or to order additional books, please write:
Dorrance Publishing Co., Inc.
701 Smithfield Street
Third Floor
Pittsburgh, Pennsylvania 15222
U.S.A.
1-800-788-7654
Or visit our web site and on-line catalog at www.dorrancepublishing.com

Acknowledgments

To Allah, who is the author and finisher of my life.

I dedicate this book to my mom, Vertelle Thompson, and my dad, Johnny Shepp.

To William Bailey, who was my first love.

Special thanks to Angela Zboray, who told me to keep writing.

To my children, Haleema Mays, Mariyam Mays, Dhaakira Mays and Mustapha Mays, who stayed up with me many long nights and supported my efforts.

To my brother Archie Shepp, who told me, "You will finish this book."

To my best friends, Evonne Hardy and Anita Branham, who allowed me to tell their stories along with mine.

To my favorite cousins, Ernestine Flournoy and Deborah Vanderhorst, who gave me many unforgettable moments growing up in Philadelphia and New York.

To my sisters, Ethel Richardson and Sharon Knox, without whose experiences this story couldn't be told.

To Joe, who taught me to love my mother through the loss of his own in a concentration camp.

To the Reverend Melvin Floyd, who opened my eyes to how brief this life is and taught me not to take it for granted.

To Reverend Cartwright, who taught me the true meaning of love through Jesus Christ.

To Mujahid Abdullah, who helped me do my research.

To the Nation of Islam and James Brown, the Godfather of Soul, who taught me self-acceptance.

To Frank Moore, who walked with me through my days during the struggle.

To Cecilie Tyson, who I heard say on the Donny Simpson Show one morning, "It's the woman's turn. If you started a book, take it out and finish it," after we were all inspired by Terry McMillian's *Waiting to Exhale*.

Special thanks to Shirley Baker and Joyce Baker Myers.

Special thanks to Roberta Shepp, who designed the cover of this book.

A banister or a couple of steps separated us from our neighbors. Houses lined our block from both sides. If you walked across from my block, there was an alley that you could walk through to get to the adjoining block. And if you wanted to get to another block, then you found another alley. If there was no alley, then you'd walk around the corner to get to another street. On every corner, there was a store, a bar, or a church. The bars didn't open on Sundays so the streets were quiet and Sundays were boring.

Like most communities in Philadelphia, we had a summer block party. Before the party actually started, we turned on the fire hydrants and washed our streets, and when the streets dried, we painted our curbs and our house numbers on the front of our houses. The city gave us long wooden flower boxes that were painted dark green to nail to the front of our banisters and a variety of colorful spring and summer flowers to accompany them. We weren't rich, but we took pride in keeping our neighborhood clean. We then celebrated our community efforts with a table spread with food and drink and music and dancing in the streets.

We had our churches, our bakery, our greasy spoons, our Jewish grocer, and we even had a movie theatre that you could see from our back window. Directly in front of my house was a building we call the Keystone. Inside this building, pieces of wood were cut to fit a mold. I never knew what the wood would later be used for, but I was informed sometime later in my life that this building was owned and operated by whites who only employed white men outside our community, which was predominately black.

This was where we gathered. When the building closed for the day, which was around five o'clock, we came back and played jacks on the steps of the Keystone, or hand games or sometimes hide-and-go-seek, the Keystone being base.

It was where at night occasionally young teenage boys would come together to sing a cappella, as if those of us who lived close to the Keystone requested some ongoing encore or something, but most of the times the boys would sing on the corner. That's how they got nicknamed The Corner Boys.

The alley next to the Keystone was where both young and old men came together, some from a hard day's work, and others just because they didn't have anything else to do but shoot craps, take a piss, or just do some cussing or small talk. Out of all of the blocks in my neighborhood, people were drawn to ours like a bee to its hive. In a way, though, I was glad because there was always some small talk, some big talk, or something going on in the hood.

This was where I dreamed and buried secrets. This was my family, my beginning, my history, and my roots. This was where I learned joy, pain, and death, sisterhood, womanhood, and passion; where I experienced my first kiss, my first love.

The day he moved in next door to my house is a day I'll always remember. He was tall, and good looking, of medium brown complexion and clean shaven, with his hair cut close. His clothes were neat and he dressed well. His voice was oh so cool, very cool and soothing. I suppose that if he was a singer he would have sung in tenor. He was laid back, and he always referred to us girls as *sista*. "Hey, sista, how ya'll doin'?" Or "My beautiful black sistas."

The Keystone

An intriguing account of the life of a young black woman growing up in inner city Philadelphia during the turbulent 1960s and early '70s. Her journey through the civil rights movement as a member of the Nation of Islam and later, the Black Panther Party, elegantly weaves together the class, economic, and race struggles that impacted black communities. **Available on:** www.amazon.com

by Anita J. Moore

The Keystone

When he said it, it made you feel good, special, pretty. No one called a black girl beautiful back in the day except when someone you knew complemented your smooth dark complexion. Even then, it was taken as an insult, so when he said it, it took us a while to digest it. When James Brown's song "Say It Loud, I'm Black and I'm Proud" first hit the charts, we sang it, but with great hesitation because we were ashamed of our color. However things were changing rapidly, so the terms *brotha* or *sista*, as we pronounced them were now held in high esteem. Love, respect, honor, admiration, reverence, sameness—the words were priceless. They linked you with your past, your present, and now your future. At one time to each other we were just another being, someone you knew who lived up the street, down the street, or around the corner, just another black face in the crowd.

This brotha could do no wrong because he called us sista, so why then did Mom believe he was on drugs and not only that, but also a drug dealer? She said that she could tell by his eyes. How? What did she see that we couldn't see? He told us we were beautiful, so how did she perceive such an evil? Then one day he invited the Corner Boys over to his house. They stayed in there for several hours, and we knew how long they had stayed because we sat on the porch the entire time to witness the whole scenario as it played out. They were never the same when they left his house, and neither was home. It would be the turning point in our lives. That's when my sister and I decided to join the struggle.

All we wanted more than anything was to save this place from an ill that would one day spread its poison throughout a community and eventually become a breeding ground for flies and maggots, feasting on the remains of what used to be home.

I asked my dad once, "Why do they call this place 'Brickyard'?" He told me that the streets used to be nothing but brick until the city converted them to asphalt. Damn! I can remember almost losing my life as my sister and I were trying to save this place from a drug dealer who came like a thief in the night, reminding me of a small cancer attaching itself to the weakness of our boys and young men and then spreading itself by feasting on the ignorance of our older men. It got so big that it consumed the minds of our men, who we looked up to, and finally it entered the spine—our women folk—and now it's in the belly. I hear that girls here and there are popping out crack babies and have created a circle of nothing but destruction and death. Just thinking about it makes me wanna holler!

Let me take you to a time we refer to as "back in the day," but first let me take you back to my beginning.

Out of all of the grades I'd been through, sixth grade was the one I remember the most. The year was 1963. My sister's friend assured me that I would like Mr. Conrad. Sis never had him for a teacher, but I prayed that I would be in his class that year and now it was finally going to happen. The year before, I had heard so much about this teacher, such as he was cool, and I would be lucky if I got him. I knew some of the girls had a schoolgirl crush on him because they expressed how fine they thought he was, how nicely he dressed and how good he always smelled.

The first day in school, we were assigned seats. Nametags were neatly taped at the top of each desk so that we knew exactly where to sit. It took about ten minutes for us to get situated before we finally sat down and folded our hands. We gave him our undivided attention as he stood before us, leaning against his desk, one leg crossed over the other leg. His hands were snuggled deep into his pockets. His shirt was neatly pressed, crispy clean and white, with no ring around the collar. He had on a tie, a tweed brown blazer, black pants, and shiny black shoes. His eyeglasses were thick though, which made his eyes appear smaller than they really were. His face was very dark and smooth, without a trace of hair.

By now the entire classroom was fragrant with the scent of his cologne. *Hmmm*, I thought to myself. I took a good look at him. *Is he fine? No*, I concluded, *but he is definitely a lady's man.* I could tell by how Miss Chauncey looked at him when she suddenly made her grand entry into the classroom, walked up to him, and whispered something in his ear. She appeared drunk with passion. She was very nicely shaped, with her hair cut short and dyed strawberry blonde. Her complexion was honey, and she wore lots of make-up to give it a smoother appearance. Her lipstick was a deep ruby red, her lips full and inviting. She had a "stick-out butt," as we called it. On this day she was wearing a beige knitted skirt, a black sweater top, stockings that matched her skin tone, and a pair of black pumps which fit her impeccably.

When we'd come home from school, Mom was either doing someone's hair, laundry, or fixing dinner. The television was on for most of the day. We only had one, a little black and white Emerson TV that had the standard coat hanger for an antenna and a pair of pliers next to the table to change the stations when we needed to. If Mom wasn't watching the soaps, then she was watching the news. She had to keep up with the civil rights movement because it was important to black people, more important than the Vietnam War. The civil rights movement had long been down in the South, I was well aware of that, but if there was a civil rights movement in the North, then I was too young to understand it.

Dad and Uncle Billy had planned on going to Washington and march with the Reverend Doctor Martin Luther King, but they ended up not going because neither of them could take off from work. Besides, I would have been scared for both of them had they gone, and when I heard that they weren't, I was glad.

I remember seeing what had happened to other black people on the television. There were dog attacks, or they were sprayed with water gushing out of long fire hoses with a force so strong that it would push back a so-called mob of people, which often included women and men, grandmothers and grandfathers, and children. Then there were black sticks striking the heads and backs of the demonstrators at the hands of racist police who carried them off to jail, and for what? Because they were black and all they wanted were equal rights, the most serious crime if you were a Negro.

I used to hear my mom singing a civil rights song called, "We Shall Overcome."

"Why do black people sing that song?" I asked.

"Well, colored people, Negroes all over the country don't have the same rights as whites," she said.

We both agreed that it was a sad song. I didn't like how it made me feel when I heard it, even to this day.

"Are the same things that happened to colored people in the South going to happen to us?" I asked. I was praying she'd say no. I didn't want to get lynched.

"Well, the South has always been open with their racism, but up here in the North, they cover it up," she said. "They don't like you, but they don't let you know it like they do in the South."

I began to dislike myself because being colored, a Negro, black, a spook, or a darkie meant that you were cursed as I had heard one of my mom's customers say. Her name was Ms. Thomas. She was a sweet lady and was sincere in what she believed. Every time she'd come over to get her hair done, she had the Good Book with her. "It's in the Old Testament of the Holy Bible," she said, "but it doesn't mean that God doesn't love us."

I couldn't figure out what that meant. How could you curse a race of people and at the same time love them? Somebody was lying. And then when we looked at the TV, all we would see were white people, pretty little white girls, and beautiful white women. What was considered beautiful? White skin and long straight hair. I never heard anybody say that black people were beautiful except for a neighbor we knew from the next block. He said that Sharon was a pretty black girl, but even then, that was an insult to her. She'd run to her room embarrassed and crying. Mom taught us not to be ashamed of our color, but why shouldn't we have been? After all, we were the cursed race.

Big Jan was Emma's mother—Jan for Janet, and Big because she was a big woman. Her skin was reddish brown, and she had thick, long, black, wavy hair that she wore in one long plait that hung like a long rope down the middle of her back. She was a Southern woman who never wore shoes in the summer. She'd walk through the alley to get to the store on pieces of glass and stone like she was walking on butter. The skin on the soles of her feet was tough like shoe leather. The tone of her voice was sort of deep, and if you blinked, then you wouldn't have understood a word she said. She talked so fast she sounded like she was speaking a different language, except for the cuss words, which were easy to decipher from the rest of the words she spoke. She amazed me every time I'd watch her from her step while Emma and I sat outside.

I loved going over to Big Jan's house, a two-story house which sat behind the rest of the row houses in our quaint, but as old as a piece of aged but good cheese, neighborhood. Thick cobwebs embellished the walls inside. It was sort of creepy, dark, gloomy, and obscure, even when the electricity was turned on. Cockroaches scurried about freely like industrious ants on a hot summer's day. The paint on the walls had long lost its color. It almost looked lifeless, except for those diligent little pests that occupied almost every part of the house. They felt creepy if they crawled on your skin.

I once looked up and saw a white one on the ceiling that looked more like a congested road map. I followed it with my eyes until a crack lead it to a whole in the wall.

"Girl, why you looking at dem roaches?" Emma asked. "Come on and git somepin' tu eat."

"But that was a white one," I said as if I had seen the most amazing creature in my life, which at that time it was. We ate our favorite food—surplus cheese and fried canned Spam. Big Jan's was a home where just about every three months you could go in the cellar and see a cat give birth to a litter of kittens; or when Big Jan wasn't home, go upstairs and peek through a keyhole and watch Ms. Gale and Ben do the nasty. There were times when every room in the house was occupied with people having sex, even in the bathroom, so I'd guard Emma if she couldn't hold her pee and had to relieve herself on the side of the house.

Every Sunday we went to Sunday school and church, although Dad never went and mom couldn't go because she never had the time—she had to do hair to help make ends meet. I remember my sister and I sometimes waking up at three or four o'clock in the morning to the smell of cleaned, pressed, and curled hair.

"Mom, why are you up so early?" we would ask, and the story was always the same. Somebody was going out of town and needed their hair fixed. But the worst part of it was that she didn't get paid until they got back. She did hair on credit, the same way we sometimes bought our food from Joe the Jewish grocer, who was tall, dark, and very handsome. He had a lovely wife named Rachel and a son named John, who Sis swore had a crush on me because every time we went to the store for our mom, he would smile and hand me a piece of candy. You couldn't have met a more compassionate family. I suppose it was because he and his wife managed to escape Hitler's camps. I saw the numbers on his arm one day and asked him if they were a tattoo. He explained to me what they were and how he got them. He also told me how his whole family perished in that camp. I could tell that he was hurting inside as he shared that part of his life with me. I felt bad for him, very bad for him.

I used to think that we were the only family who bought food on credit. I didn't want anybody to know, so when Mom gave me a note, which included the words "Will pay later," I'd wait until everybody left the store before I handed it to him. Before Joe left the neighborhood, I discovered that just about everybody bought food on credit. He knew what it was like to have to struggle, so he had an understanding with the community. His motto was, "Feed your family now, pay later when you can afford to." He would always say, "Love your mother, be good to your mother, love your mother." God bless you and your family forever, Joe.

My mom was the kind of person who didn't like to let anybody down. She was always dedicated to her work, but she encouraged us to go to church. She believed that going to church would keep us from sinning and keep us out of trouble. There were only a handful of members, and only three people sang in the choir. Reverend Shane was our pastor, although he looked to be about a hundred years old. His wife was a tall, light-skinned woman who looked to be about twenty-five years younger than he was, and his only daughter was tall, brown, shapely, and very beautiful to everybody. She was also the church's pianist. Reverend Shane was one of the nicest men I knew.

After services ended, he would say in a voice so shaky that it was barely audible, "Okay boys and girls, come and get your candy." That's how he always got us to come back the next Sunday, and to us that was the best part about going to church—getting your candy. Everything else was boring until Reverend Carter came to take his place since Reverend Shane was soon to retire. I was surprised to see a young preacher standing in the pulpit preaching that Sunday's sermon because all of the preachers who came before him were old men. We felt a strong connection with this man because of his humility and child-like spirit.

I had experienced a lot of unhappiness in my life because my dad drank, like a lot of fathers in the `hood, but this man was always sober, always happy, and it was blowing my mind. I used to think that being a Christian meant that you always had to be sad because of the sad-faced image of a white Jesus that stared you in the eye from the pulpit and the depressing songs the choir always struggled to sing.

When Reverend Carter stood up to preach, his words fell like drops of rain on a dry and thirsty congregation who hadn't tasted water for a long time, and for the first time I understood what it meant to be a true Christian.

The Lyric was the name of the movie theatre that sat behind our house. A wall separated everybody's house from the theatre, but that didn't keep the Corner Boys from climbing it and sneaking in through the back to catch a free movie. It only cost twenty-five cents to get in, and the same movie played all day and night. If your mom let you, then you could watch it a couple of times during that day. New movies didn't come out as often as they do now.

The Lyric and the Uptown, which was the rock and roll show, were our only sources of entertainment. Oh, another one was the Penny-R-Kay, where people would hang out and take pictures, but we never went because we never had any money to take pictures or to ride the trolley down town.

On Saturdays we were given a card, which had about ten numbers on it, upon leaving the theatre. On the following Saturday, there was always a big blackboard in the lobby of the theatre, which had numbers on it, too. If any one of your numbers matched a number on this board, then you got in for free.

The Lyric was my second home, next to Emma's house. It was also where I was fingered by a pervert in my neighborhood after not listening to my mom when she said, "Stay away from strangers." He asked me to take his daughter to the bathroom, and I responded hastily with a "yes" because I knew that I would most likely get some extra money for doing him a favor. However when we got back, he wanted me to sit down next to him for awhile. *Nobody will miss me*, I thought to myself, because I won't be that long. It didn't take long before he had his hand on my thigh, then in my underwear. "You like that?" he asked. But I couldn't move. I couldn't talk. All I wanted to do was throw up.

He then removed his hand from my private area and put it in his pocket. He took out a dirty quarter and placed it gently in my hand. "Now don't tell anybody," he said. "It's our secret." I felt ashamed as I left the theatre, running all the way home. I got in the tub and tried to wash away my guilt, but that's something you can't wash away. I wanted to tell somebody but it made me feel dirty just to talk about it. About a year later he was accused of raping a six-year-old girl and then placing her almost lifeless body under a rug in an old abandoned house.

The Lyric was a also a place and time when East met West. We lived on the East side of Brickyard and as I mentioned before, most of us on that side were black. Only a handful of residents were Italians. Italians and Jews used to dominate the West side, but today it has become mostly black, too. We never fought with the West side. Blacks sat with blacks and whites sat with whites in the theatre, but eventually we would fight one another, black against black!

We had been in school now for several weeks. Before classes started we would always line up outside in the schoolyard in rows, resembling little brown soldiers in military camp, and Mrs. Holden, the school's new principal, looked like some kind of drill sergeant. She was of German decent, very tall and pale, of medium build with blonde hair and blue eyes. You wouldn't find a trace of make-up on her face, and she always dressed in all black or gray. Her wedge-heeled shoes had military look about them and they squeaked with every step she took. She had a key ring that looked like it contained a thousand keys, and when it was time for us to get ready to enter the building for class, she would blow the whistle that was attached to it. At that point, everyone had to freeze, just stop whatever we were doing at that moment.

One day a boy named Keith was playing with a girl named Anna. When Mrs. Holden blew the whistle, he stumbled and fell on top of her. It looked like they were "doing it." The funny thing was that they had to stay in that position until she blew the whistle a second time. We tried our best to hold in our laughter, which by this time wasn't easy. This happened in the back of the schoolyard, so Miss Holden didn't know what was going on. Had she known, then we would have been hit with the lickety-stick. We weren't supposed to say or do anything when she blew her whistle.

I remember this particular day when she blew her whistle, and everybody went silent. Michael, who was a student in my class, had a cold. He coughed up a glob of phlegm and spit it on the ground. It was so quiet in the schoolyard that Mrs. Holden heard the spit hit the ground. She demanded that the person responsible speak up, "Right this instant!" she shouted. He confessed that it was him. She then marched right up to him and demanded that he get on all fours and wipe it up with his hand, then she made him wipe the disgusting slime on his shirt.

I remember she smiled on only three occasions. The first time was when she was involved in conversation between herself and faculty members. The second time was when she was addressing parents at a PTA meeting. And the third occasion was the one I'll never forget. She walked with her head held high like a first class lieutenant adorned with medals of honor, jingling her one thousands keys, then purposely dropping them on the ground. Wherever she was standing at that point little brown boys and girls scrambled toward her feet, knocking each other out of the way, hoping to be the first one to pick them up before gently placing them back in her hand. If you succeeded, then she'd reward you with a smile. In retrospect, I can clearly see now that our principal was, plainly and simply, a racist who got pleasure out of seeing little brown boys and girls step and fetch as she strutted with an air of superiority throughout the entire school.

An operation to remove varicose veins had made its entry into the medical field and they needed a guinea pig, so they asked my mom if she would volunteer and she agreed. She would be the first person ever to undergo such a procedure where an incision over the skin of each vein was made and then the vein was surgically removed. Mom was excited, and we were just as excited because the doctors said that she was making medical history being the first person ever to have this procedure done, and plus her name would appear in the medical books.

She had the worst kind of varicose veins, the thick ones which covered her feet, legs, and thighs, but I never recalled her ever being embarrassed about her legs. I remember the few times when she would dress up to go somewhere, and I mean few because my mom was such a homebody. She was a hairdresser, and she even did her customer's hair in our house because my dad didn't want her to work outside the house. He believed that a mother's place was in the home.

My mom liked wearing black dresses to give her full figure a more slender look. She would then color her shapely full lips a deep red that was almost burgundy to complement her brown complexion. She didn't need anything else on her face. To me she was just naturally beautiful—even her legs were beautiful, in spite of the veins because when I'd see them, I was reminded that her condition was caused from bearing children, the children she loved so much that sometimes she would stand up all day and night, which was more stress on her legs. Sometimes she would be on her feet until three or even four in the morning, pressing hair while we slept so that she could help dad keep a roof over our heads and food on the table.

Even though mom was in the hospital, we still went to school. Mr. Conrad had divided our class into three groups: alpha, beta, and gamma. Alpha was the above average group all the kids eventually called "the smart group." Your grade average had to be an A or B. Beta was the average group, in which you had a B or C average. Gamma was the below average group, which the kids in the classroom called "the dumb group." Because you had a D or below D average. I didn't think I was dumb at the time, but that's the group I was placed in. It left me with a complex.

I could already tell that Evelyne, who was a white girl, and Brenda, who was a black girl, would be Mr. Conrad's pets. Evelyne was already wearing make-up and I heard that this was her third time being in the sixth grade. She and Brenda were fully developed and more mature than the rest of us, who were mostly ten and eleven, while they were thirteen. Maybe that's why Mr. Conrad singled out the two of them to be his pets. I began to feel that a girl had to look like a woman and have big titties if you wanted to be his pet, and if that were the case, I'd never be one.

Emma was in Mrs. Reed's class. Mrs. Reed was short with dark brown curly hair and looked to be in her early to mid-fifties.

Her face was always red, and so were her eyes. She always smelled like whiskey, but I always thought that it was mouthwash until the kids in school said that it was whiskey I smelled. It was hard for me to conceive that a teacher would actually come to school drunk until she bent over one day to pick something up off the floor and a fifth of vodka fell out of her pocketbook. Nobody ever told the principal, but all the kids in the school laughed under their breath every time she walked by.

Mrs. Reed was the L.D. teacher, which meant "learning disability." Emma's mom couldn't read or write and therefore wasn't able to help her with her schoolwork. She struggled to teach herself, so she was therefore assumed to be a slow learner. Back then, L.D. was called O.B. We never knew what O.B. meant, but the children used to say that O.B. meant "out of brains," so whoever was in Mrs. Reed's class was said to be "out of brains."

The kids in her class were never given any homework and most of their day was spent drawing pictures. Very little reading, writing, and math were given to them. Some of the kids in the class were mentally retarded. It was messed up, because Emma was bright but overlooked and was not given the extra help she needed, as was the case with some of the other kids in her class because they were black and poor like the rest of us.

John F. Kennedy was the president. One particular morning Mr. Conrad left the classroom in a haste and then returned as abruptly as he left. However only when he came back, he was crying. He removed his thick glasses and wiped away his tears. He looked at the class as if he was waiting for one of us to ask him why he was crying, but no one dared ask. "The president has been shot dead," he said. I could tell that the class was deeply affected by what they had just heard, and as the news began to sink in, I looked around the classroom. Tears were rolling down the faces of my classmates, but I couldn't cry. I tried to fake it but couldn't. Everybody said that Kennedy was for the black people. People said it in my neighborhood, even people who lived in my house and people who came to get their hair done, but I never saw him in any of the marches. My dad worked two jobs that didn't come close to paying the bills and I never knew of any black person in my entire neighborhood who even came close to being well off. If I had to shed my tears for anybody that day, it would have been for my mother.

Several weeks had gone by since the tragic death of President Kennedy and by this time things weren't right in Mr. Conrad's class. I knew what it meant to be the teacher's pet, but where does teacher draw the line? The relationship between Mr. Conrad, Evelyne, and Brenda was sometimes so physical we would forget that Evelyne and Brenda were students at all, and we could clearly see that both of them had a crush on him. They seemed to be more like his secretaries, especially Evelyne. We'd sit and stare while he took turns grabbing Evelyne and Brenda around the bosoms and then press his body against their buttocks, or he'd take them behind a partition he had set up in the back of the classroom. We'd then hear a lot of giggling and kissing. Most of the physical contact was between Evelyn and Mr. Conrad though.

He seemed to be prepping her to become his woman. It was as though he was playing a mind game with her by making her feel like an adult. That way he could justify his actions so that neither he nor she would feel any guilt about what they were doing, and it seemed to be working. She was given the privilege of disciplining the class and grading papers. He even gave her a desk identical to his!

One day he emerged from behind the partition holding Evelyne by the hand and said, "Hey, class, Evelyne's discovered a new way to say 'six.' She says, 'sex.' He thought it was funny, so we thought it was funny, too. I didn't care how she pronounced the word "six." All I cared about was trying to get As like she got for doing nothing.

I went to Big Jan's house after school since I didn't have any homework that day. The house was full like it was most of the time, with folks drinking, cussing, and playing cards. If a door was closed, then somebody was "doing the nasty," as Emma and I referred to it. We'd take turns peeking through the keyhole.

Big Jan's boyfriend was always admiring Emma's legs. Emma was light-skinned but she was also very hairy. He always seemed to have this fascination for her legs. He'd stare at them for awhile and then say, "Emma takes care of her legs." Emma and I hated him. He drank all the time and he was mean. He wouldn't let her use the bathroom when everybody was using the rooms in the house, including the bathroom. We'd sit around grown folks for a while, laughing at the winos and watching them play card games.

The electricity was finally turned back on after two months of being turned off. During the time it was off, Emma and I would go upstairs in her bedroom when no one was home and play with her blonde-haired blue-eyed Barbie doll. Barbie wasn't Asian, Black, or Hispanic back then, but she was the image of what we saw as the beautiful white woman. We played until the night consumed the three of us. We were having so much fun that I never realized how dark it had gotten. When we could no longer see Barbie, then I knew that it was time to go home. I got away with going over to Big Jan's house as much as I did because my mom was always doing hair. Had she known where I'd been, then I would have been in big trouble. She knew what went on in there, so I was restricted from going over to her house. However I was there so much everybody in Big Jan's house knew my name, and Emma and I began to give them nicknames based on their characteristics. Eventually the whole neighborhood called them by those names.

So it was with this particular lady we called Sarah, but we nicknamed her Tip-toes because every time she got drunk she would walk on the tips of her toes. She was scared that she was going to fall. She was a tall, thin woman with a tan complexion, and her jet black hair stood up on her head all the time. She wore very thick glasses and only had three teeth in her mouth, one fang at the top right side and two at the bottom on either side. She got a laugh out of us calling her tip-toes. I also recall another woman in our neighborhood who was a heavy drinker and who loved Stevie Wonder's song "Uptight," so Sharon used to call her "Uptight" and she loved it. Sometimes when we were on the third floor of our house we could hear her singing as she walked down the street. One of us would jump up and yell from the window, "Uptight!"

She'd respond, "Everything's all right!"

Then we'd say, "Jesus!" and she'd say, "Yes, Lord."

Then we'd say, "Talk about it!" and she'd say, "Don't shout it!" We even had the grown-ups doing it.

Ms. Robin was the neighborhood gossip. We loved hanging around the shop when she was there because she was always running her mouth about somebody else's business. Her favorite one-liner when she was about to drop a bombshell was, "Honey, let me tell you." Then smacking her lips and looking up at my mother with her very large eyes and a face that was plump and brown and pretty, she'd drop the bomb. She either had us all laughing or Mom saying, "Whaaaat?" or "Girl, hush yo' moth, for truth?" Most of the time Mom made us leave the shop when she came over because her gossip was too much for our little ears.

Every Sunday we watched Shirley Temple on the television. She was the idol of every little black girl in my neighborhood. When Easter rolled around, every one of us wanted Shirley Temple curls to dangle on our foreheads. My hair was long so I considered myself to be lucky. You couldn't tell me that I wasn't a little wanna-be version of the little white girl I idolized so much.

Our church had grown from twenty-five members to about fifty members since Reverend Carter took over as pastor. Reverend Carter was always happy, always smiling. I couldn't help but praise this man every chance I got. As far as I was concerned, he was a black angel sent from heaven to us. I didn't know of any other black man in my neighborhood who could ever fit into his mold. He had young ideas. I wanted what he had, and that was joy every time we came together. It was like receiving the candy that

Reverend Shane used to give us after Sunday school. We even started a young people's choir since we loved to sing. Reverend Carter talked to us about baptism and what it meant to be a Christian, so I decided that I wanted to get baptized.

During the week, though, I had to deal with what was going on in my classroom and the longer I remained a student in Mr. Conrad's class, the more inferior I began to feel because he had a way of calling gammas stupid if we made a mistake or didn't understand something. So I never raised my hand, even when I knew the answer to a question. He would stress the last three letters of the word stupid and drag it out so that the sound would be long and high-pitched, like, stup*iiii*d! Alphas and Betas would laugh at us, and we felt degraded.

The day my mom had her operation was also the day I was supposed to bring in two new composition books. I was the only one who was unprepared and I grew more nervous as I looked around the room on everyone else's desk, hoping that perhaps I had missed someone who might also be unprepared like myself, but as it turned out, I was the only one. Mr. Conrad walked over to my desk and we looked each other straight in the eye. "Where are your books?" he asked in a calm voice.

"I don't have any," I said. I felt my eyes fill with tears as much as I tried to hold them back. I didn't want to get called stupid in front of the whole class, and at this point, all eyes were on me. All I wanted to do at that moment was disappear.

"Why don't you have your books?" he asked.

"My mom is in the hospital getting an operation on her legs, and my dad didn't have time to buy them from the store."

He walked away from my desk and walked over to his, then opened his desk drawer and took out two new books. He walked back toward my desk and handed me the two new books. I said thank you and he said, "You're welcome." I thought to myself as I smiled, *Maybe he ain't that bad after all.*

My mom didn't stay in the hospital long. Before the operation, we were told that she would be in the medical books as the first person ever to undergo such a procedure and that she was making medical history. We were even told that she would make the big news, so for several days we sat and watched the television and checked the paper, but there was no mention of it, not even in the local paper. The operation wasn't a success because it was the first of its kind and had not been perfected yet, but it wasn't long before she was back on her two feet doing hair.

A new girl came to our class one particular day. She was cute and light skinned with short, pressed, curled hair and a smile that was as contagious as yawning. I heard from some of the other kids in the class that she had just been given back to her mother after coming out of foster care. Her name was Stella, but we called her by her nickname, which was Misty. I didn't know any other details regarding this girl, but I did know that if you were a foster child, there was a problem in your home, and I'm certain that Mr. Conrad knew something of her background.

It wasn't long before she complained about Mr. Conrad playing favorites. She didn't like him and he didn't like her either, but she was street smart, not naive like the rest of us. She used to observe Mr. Conrad when he was behind the partition doing his thing while telling me stories of her and different boys she did it with. Misty couldn't keep her eyes off of Mr. Conrad. I figure he knew that she suspected what was going on, so whenever she was in the classroom he'd be more meticulous about his relationships with Evelyne and Brenda.

Eventually Brenda stopped coming to school. We were told that her mom had died and that she and her dad moved away. Misty's hatred toward Mr. Conrad had continued to grow, especially because he continued to give Evelyne more and more attention and the rest of us less attention. Misty had a name she used to call him—"ol' black crispy critter." We would laugh because insulting someone who was very dark by calling them degrading names was funny back then in our days of ignorance. Then one day he unthinkingly took Evelyne behind the partition and we heard a lot of giggling, then kissing. "He ain't got no business kissing no chald! I'ma tell," she said tapping her pencil on her desk.

The velocity it took that rumor to spread seemed like a twinkling of an eye. The next thing we knew, the authorities were in our classroom later on that week, and things didn't look good for Mr. Conrad. He was extremely nervous. We heard that Misty was being held somewhere for questioning, and we didn't see her at school anymore.

Mr. Conrad took that as an opportunity to talk to us individually. This is what he said to me: "Do you know why Stella was put in a foster home?"

"No," I said nervously as I looked into his eyes through his very thick glasses.

"She was a troublemaker and she told lies about people she didn't like," he said. He spoke slowly and with clarity as he continued to defend himself. "She won't be coming back to school, but instead, she's going back to a home. If you say things like she did, then you'll go to a home, too," he said.

I didn't want to go to a home, so he frightened me when he said that. The authorities came back again, and this time they questioned us, wanting to know what a normal class day was like.

"We draw pictures and we go to recess; we read and study math," we all took turns telling about things that went on in the classroom, but made no mention of Mr. Conrad's sexual relationship with Eveylne and Brenda. None of us wanted to be taken away from our homes like Misty.

Mr. Conrad wasn't present during the questioning, but when I got home, Mom asked the same questions. She had heard about the rumors too, and I gave her the same answers. Evelyn left the school, and I never knew what happened to her after that, but Mr. Conrad changed and took more interest in the rest of us. He was also nicer and stopped calling us stupid. He even took some of us out of gamma group and put us in beta. I was one of them, but I used to wonder if it was because I had improved or if it was because I didn't tell.

I was finally baptized and I felt like I understood what it was to be a Christian and follow Jesus Christ. I understood that baptism meant that you were making a public statement to everyone you knew that your life would be different from now on. Being baptized meant that "Behold, old things were passed away and all things were new." It also meant that I couldn't go over to Big Jan's house anymore. That thought used to play over and over again in my head, but at the same time I couldn't back out now. I had chosen baptism over going to Big Jan's house, but I would have to deal with that later.

Sharon wasn't ready yet. I used to think that she was keeping deep dark secrets from me, but she sincerely expressed that she just wasn't sure if she could keep such a commitment. She was doing the right thing, and I just hoped that I was, too. I loved Jesus, but I also loved going over Big Jan's house.

My mom came to my baptism, which meant a lot to me. She didn't go to church because she was always doing hair. I remember her coming to church only one other time, so this would be the second time. I felt like I was blessed for getting baptized because God was giving me a second chance to do the right things in life, and for the first time, I knew God was real. Now I knew why Reverend Carter was happy all the time. Thanks, Mom, for coming to my baptism. I love you.

It's funny how you feel so grown-up when you're going into the seventh grade. I felt like I had already matured by five years when I saw seventh grade stamped on my report card.

Summer had finally kicked in. I loved summer because we had our summer block parties and once a year we went to Atlantic City with our church. Back then, there were no casinos, just the boardwalk where you could buy lots of things with very little cash, and then there was the beach and lots of rides—my favorite was the giant Ferris wheel.

The highlight of our summers was when our cousins came to visit us from New York. This year our cousin Debbie was coming first. As soon as she stepped out of the cab, she'd say,

"Hi, chicklets." That's how we would greet one another and then we would laugh. She had lived with us until she was seven. We would play house and she would always be the mom. She would get celery and carrots from her mother's fridge and that's what we had for dinner, then chicklets were for dessert.

Debbie was closer to Sharon's age, so they spent a lot of time together, but people thought that Debbie and I were sisters because we were the same complexion and were skinny with thick plaits that came to our shoulders. She was the peacemaker as my mother would sometimes call her because she always had this yearning for peace and happiness. She felt like everybody could get along with one another if they just put forth some effort and tried to get to know each other.

We used to fight with these two sisters who had just moved four row houses down the street from us. We never told them what our names were because we didn't like how they looked. As far as we were concerned, they thought that they were hard, tough, and all that, so when Debbie came to our house, we tried to get her to dislike them too, but she told us that we were silly not to like someone we never met. I recall being mad because she didn't feel the same way about them as we did. She went down to their house and asked them if they would come outside. Sharon and I just stood there watching. We fought with these sisters all the time, and now Debbie was making an effort to finally stop the feuding between us, so we respected her because she had a level of maturity that we had not yet reached. She made us shake hands and introduce ourselves. I felt awkward at first, but at the same time the whole scenario made me laugh and just like that, everything mellowed out. To this day, Cherylanne and Patricia are like my blood sisters.

Debbie was growing up. She wore her hair differently now, not like mine which was still in braids, and by now her breasts were very visible. She came in the house and hugged Mom. They talked a bit about how her mom was doing, then we took her upstairs to put away her things. I would glance at her breasts every now and then because they were big and I was still flat chested. "You got a big chest," I said.

"Yours haven't started to grow yet?" she asked.

"No I mean, how do you know when you are starting to grow breasts?" I asked.

She lifted my blouse and grabbed the skin around my nipple, then she took my hand and told me to do the same. "Feel that lump?" she asked.

"Yeah," I said.

"You're getting breasts," she said. I was happy and started laughing.

"You got your menstruation?" she asked.

"What's that?" we asked.

"You don't know what a period is?"

"No," we said. So she taught us things about growing up that we didn't know. What we learned back then we learned from the streets or someone else told us. Our mom didn't speak of those things until they happened. It wasn't until girls started getting pregnant at a very young age that sex education was incorporated into the school system.

The Beatles were a hot group, and their songs were cute and catchy. In our home we listened to a variety of music—jazz, blues, rock and roll—and groups such as the Temptations, the Four Tops, Smokey Robinson and the Miracles, the Supremes, Martha and the Vandellas, James Brown, Marvin Gaye, Elvis, Ray Charles, and so many others. The Beatles were on a lot of radio stations because they were making a lot of hits and so we listened to them, too. The movie *A Hard Day's Night* was playing at the Lyric, so we went to see it with Cherylanne and Patricia. We all had our favorite Beatle—Debbie liked Paul, Emma liked George, Sharon liked John, and I liked Ringo, but Cherylanne and Patricia loved Smokey.

The Lyric was packed that Saturday with little white girls. We were the only black girls there that day. We had on Beatle sneakers we bought from the five-and-dime store for fifty cents, shorts, and white blouses. The fellas were on the corner laughing at us because we were going to see the Beatles. I used to think that they were just jealous, but to them it was also strange that black girls back then would think that these white boys with long hair and British accents were cool.

We were near the front of the line, so we got good seats. When the Beatles came on the screen, all you heard was screaming. The white girls had caught Beatlemania. That's when they would lose control of themselves and start screaming and crying. Debbie caught Beatlemania and nearly tore off Patricia's blouse in the theatre. It looked like it had gone through a shredder, and we laughed all the way home because we had to hold her blouse together until she went into the house. Debbie stayed with us for about four weeks before she had to go back to New York. Before she left, she taught us how to two-step, or slow dance, so that when we would be allowed to go to parties, we would know how to slow dance with a boy. She also taught me how to do my own hair. Two weeks later I went to New York to visit my other cousin Nadine since she wouldn't be coming to Philadelphia this summer. I would also be visiting my brother. A neighbor by the name of Mr. Robert was going to visit some friends and my mom asked if he wouldn't mind taking me with him and dropping me off at her sister's house. Mr. Robert was cool. He was very fond of my mom and never hesitated to do her a favor. Back when I was young, New York seemed to be this far, far away place, but from Philadelphia it was only an hour and a half drive. I slept until we got to the Lincoln Tunnel because I suffered from motion sickness and I knew I would have thrown up if I had stayed awake.

Nadine's mother and my mother were sisters. Her father was from Honduras. She was what black people considered pretty with "good hair" because she was "high yellow" and her hair was long, black, and wavy. Nadine was the opposite of Debbie, and since we were closer in age, we were together more than she and Sharon.

I knocked on the door. "Well, look at you," she said.

"You got skinny, Nadine. Do you eat?" I asked.

"Yeah, I eat, I'm just thin."

She wore her hair in two long braids.

"Your hair grew too," I said.

"Ma! Come in the bedroom," she said. "I want you to say hi to Mom. Ma, Nita is here."

Looking at my aunt was like looking at my mother.

"Hi, Aunt Josephine," I said.

"Come over here and give me a big hug," she said. "You doing good in school?" she asked.

"Yeah, I'm doing okay." I said.

"And how's your mother and everybody else at your house?" she asked.

"They're all doing fine," I said. I was glad to see my aunt. I hadn't seen her in a couple of years and so this summer was extra special to me, but I saw her for only one day because by the next day, she was out playing cards. My aunt loved playing cards. Sometimes a card game might last for several days at a time since everybody was trying to win back their money. Nadine had six brothers, but she was the only girl.

One of her brother's friends came over the following day. He looked to be about fourteen or fifteen years old, but he had the body and mind of a more mature young man. He was light brown in complexion and not bad looking. He kept staring at me from the time he entered the house. We sat around and got a game of cards going, and he wanted to sit next to me at the table. He told me I was cute, but I didn't like the way he was looking at me. He made me feel uncomfortable and now since my auntie wasn't there, I was feeling really insecure.

I had to use the bathroom, so I excused myself from the card game. Smokey Robinson's song "You Really Got a Hold on Me" was playing. I went upstairs and closed the door behind me, but when I came out, he was standing outside the door. I started to go back down the stairs but he would stop me whenever I tried. "You wanna wrestle?" he asked.

I tried to laugh it off and said, "No," but I was scared. The music was loud and no one could hear me. He backed me into my cousin's bedroom and pushed me down onto a bare mattress. We all slept on bare mattresses because there were never enough sheets to go around.

He grabbed my hands and placed them above my head as he lay on top of me. I kept begging him to let me up, but he was too strong. My strength was nothing against his. Then he took both of my hands and held them with his right hand while he commenced to unbutton my blouse with his left. He opened my pants and then he opened his. He pulled down his pants and I started screaming as loud as I could. "What the fuck are you doing to my cousin?" I looked over at one of Nadine's brothers. Those were the sweetest words I had heard all that day, even sweeter than Smokey's song, which was my favorite at the time.

"Get the fuck out of here and don't come back," he said. He got up and left. I was crying and fixing my blouse. "Are you all right?" he asked.

"Yeah, I'm all right," I said. In the meantime, Nadine was laughing at me because she thought it was funny. I tried to laugh it off, but I was embarrassed.

"Come me to the park," she said. That's how she would say, "come with me,"—"come me."

"Do you smoke?" she asked. I was twelve at the time and she was eleven.

"Yeah," I said. She pulled out a pack of Salems and gave me one. She lit my cigarette, then hers, and we started smoking. She looked at me and started laughing. "What's so funny?" I asked.

"You're not smoking," she said. "You're puffin. Smoking is when you inhale."

"What do you mean?" I asked.

"Watch this," she said. She took in some smoke and inhaled it down her throat. "Now you try it." I did as I was told.

"Hey, that's right. You did good for your first time. I choked the first time I tried it," she said. She let me have what was left in the pack, then she pulled out a pack of paper and something that looked like dried-up grass and started rolling up her own cigarettes.

"What's that?" I asked.

"Reefa," she said. "You don't know what this is yet, so you just keep smoking them cigarettes for now. You're not ready for this. You see, when you smoke this, you never let the smoke out. Watch." She talked as though she was very experienced at this. She held the smoke in, being very careful not to let any of it escape from her mouth. Her light skin was now turning slightly red, but she continued until she finished the whole thing. After she finished her "reefa," as she called it, we went back to her house. I was feeling sick and needed to lie down. She said that I was feeling sick because it was my first time smoking.

I stayed at my aunt's house a couple more days and then we took the train to my brother's apartment. My brother is a jazz player, and at the time he lived in Greenwich Village.

People in the Village were a lot different than people living in Harlem. They dressed differently and even acted differently. A lot of them looked like hippies. It was like entering another world.

My brother lived on the third floor of this big apartment building, and Nadine was inquisitive, so after we were there for a couple of days, she wanted to explore the streets and then visit one of my brother's friends who lived downstairs. We had heard that he was living with two sisters who were white, while he was black. I never saw black and white couples together until I visited the Village.

We knocked on his door and he told us to come in. He was sitting down on the floor, but you could easily tell by the length of his legs and the size of his feet that he was a very tall man. He had a dark complexion with long, coarse, matted hair that hung from his head like stalks of black wool. I was later told that he had dreadlocks. I'd never seen or heard of them before either. We told him who we were and that we had wanted to meet him. He was very pleasant and told us to sit down and make ourselves at home. His pad, as they called it, was small but quaint.

The two sisters, who were both on their knees, stopped biting off his crusty toenails to turn around and say hello. They looked very similar to one another. Even their hair looked the same, which was dark brown and curly. They then continued to chew away at his crusty toenails, but we got up and left in a hurry because we could no longer hold in our laughter. People in the Village were really weird!

Later on that night we went up on the roof and sat down on milk crates. "Are you a virgin?" she asked.

"I don't know what the word 'virgin' means," I said.

"For real, Nita?" she asked. "You don't know what a virgin is?" She was asking as if she was feeling sorry for me. "Dang, girl," she said, "you don't know nothing. It's when you never did it before with a boy." I didn't know how to answer her. I thought that if I told her that I was, then she would start laughing and making fun of me, so instead I turned the tables and asked her if she was. She never answered my question but instead she said, "When you get a boyfriend, make sure he has bow legs, not scissor legs."

"What's scissor legs?" I asked.

"Knocked knees," she said. "A bow-legged man will keep you open all night long." Then she started laughing like she always did. Like I mentioned before, we weren't taught sex education in school. What we learned, we learned from each other.

We got bored and decided to go outside to buy balloons. When we got back we filled them with water and took them with us back on the roof. As people walked by, we threw them on their heads. This one guy actually thought that it was raining. "Oh my God, it's raining," he said. Then he started dancing around in circles with his hands up in the air. We were cracking up.

We continued to throw balloons until we heard banging on the door below us, and we knew we were in trouble. My brother tried to keep his composure, but I could tell that he was angry.

"Were you throwing water balloons off of the roof?" he asked. We couldn't lie because our clothes were wet and fragments of colorful pieces of thin rubber lay on the ground below us.

"Yeah, but we're sorry," we said. We then said we wouldn't do it again. We sounded like two five-year-olds, but my brother wasn't having it. He said that he was sending Nadine home in a cab the next morning. I pouted and she cried like a baby.

After she left, there really wasn't anything much to do. My brother took me out one day because he had some running around to do. It was windy outside. I mean the hawk was really kicking.

"Did you ever see a movie star before?" he asked.

"No," I said.

"Look over across the street," he said.

It was Sidney Poitier! I yelled to him across the street to please let me have his autograph, but he said that he had a plane to catch. "Another time," he said. I was disappointed, because the next time I'd see him again would be in a movie.

If I wasn't going anywhere with my brother, then I'd go on the fire escape and smoke a cigarette when he wasn't around or just stare at the hippies and listen to the sounds of Archie Shepp. I didn't know that much about hippies except that they wanted the war to end. They'd hold demonstrations and wore symbols that represented peace and love, like peace signs and flowers. I heard that they wanted to go back to a natural state of mind, which meant a natural way of living. That meant no chemicals in their foods. I had read they had their own farms and would rather suffer the pains of giving birth to their babies than numb their bodies. Why would somebody want to feel pain? That was one of the reasons why I called them weird. They even gave their babies breast milk. I thought at the time only animals did that. I used to think that their way of life was kind of barbaric, but I was on the outside looking in. Being black meant staying with your own kind and the civil rights movement, so I never saw a black hippie in my world and to me they were just a group of disillusioned white folks who were fed up with their system but also liked the attention they were receiving from the media.

My mom used to say that one day they were going to wash their hair, cut it, put on business suits, and get all the good jobs, maybe even own some of the companies. She said that they were just going through a phase and that they were angry with the white establishment, which included the FBI and the CIA and J. Edgar Hoover, and this was their way of rebelling against an establishment that promoted war with Vietnam, racism, and hatred of black people. They didn't want to be associated with middle class or upper class white America anymore, so they lived a life that sanctified them from the rest of white America.

I returned home four weeks later. Philadelphia looked so much smaller in comparison to New York. I saved some cigarettes because I was going to teach Sharon and Emma how to smoke. Sharon and I used to go downstairs sometimes late at night after Mom did hair and drink leftover beer from her customer's glasses and puff on cigarette butts, but now I was going to show her how to inhale.

I hugged my mom and filled her in on how everybody was doing in New York. She was doing hair as usual. "How's my sister?" she asked.

"She's fine," I said. "She still likes to play cards." She started to laugh. Then I ran upstairs to see Sharon. Dad was still asleep because he had to get up later and go to work.

Sharon was lying across the bed reading an Archie comic book.

"What did you do in New York? I know you and Nadine found some trouble to get into, I just know y'all did," she said jokingly.

"Yeah," I said. "We bombed some people with water balloons from the roof over at Vernon's house and he caught us. It was so funny. He was sitting on the fire escape the whole time. He wouldn't let Nadine stay after that. She had to go home. Guess what?" I asked.

"What?" she asked.

"Two things. I saw Sidney Poitier in person!"

"No you didn't," she said.

"Yes I did. Vernon was taking me to the store and he said, 'Did you ever see a movie star in person before?'

I said no, then he said, 'Look across the street.' Then I said, 'Oh! Sidney Poitier! Can I get his autograph?' He said that I could. He looked like he was in a rush to go somewhere. I called his name and he looked at me and smiled. 'Can I have your autograph, please?' I asked. Then you know how he talked in *Lilies of the Field?* He said, 'I can't. I have a plane to catch. I'm telling you the truth. If you don't believe me, then call Vernon and ask him."

"Don't worry," she said. "I will."

"And promise you won't tell this one."

"I promise," she said.

"I'm smoking now. Nadine showed me how. Remember how we used to take a cigarette out of the ashtray when Mom's customer would leave one burning, and how we thought we were smoking? That wasn't smoking. We were puffin'."

I took a half a pack of cigarettes from my pocket. "Crack the window," I said. "Watch this." I lit the cigarette and drew in some smoke. "See," I said, holding in the smoke. Then I let it out.

"Show me," she said, as if she were pleading.

"Okay, but I'm telling you now, later on you'll probably get sick, but only for awhile. Your body has to get used to it." I handed her the cigarette.

"Like this?" she asked.

"Yeah, that's it. Finish it and then throw the butt in the trash."

"Where are you gonna get cigarettes after you finish that pack?" she asked. "You ain't got no money and no job."

"I'm gonna get them off the street. People are throwing away almost a whole cigarette. I'll bag some one day, and you do it the next day. Then when we get our allowance, we'll put our money together and buy a pack. Picture that," I said, smiling.

"It sounds good to me," she said.

So that's what we did when we couldn't afford to buy cigarettes. We took turns and bagged butts in brown paper bags and smoked them on the third floor of our house.

"What's everybody been doing?" I asked.

"Partying," she said.

"And what about church?" I asked. "Is everybody still going to church?"

"No," she said. "Nobody wants to go anymore. Everybody's losing interest. Partying is more fun."

I lit another cigarette, then there was a bit of silence. "What are you thinking about?" I asked.

"You won't get mad if I say this, will you?" she said.

"No, what?" I said. "Say it."

"I used to be jealous of you."

"Me? Why?"

"Because of your complexion and your hair was always long."

"Yeah, but Mom's customers always call you the pretty one. They never say that about me. They say that I got pretty eyes. That's about it. And you were always Daddy's favorite. You're his first-born daughter. You know, like Daddy's little girl. I always felt that he liked you more because y'all were the same complexion."

"I never felt that coming from him," she said.

"Well, you had to be me to feel it," I said.

"I like this guy who lives up the street."

"Who?" I asked.

"One of the Johnsons," she said.

"Which one?" I asked.

"Tony," she said.

"Ooh, the fine one," I said. "He likes you, too?" I asked.

"Yeah, so I hear."

"Does Mom know?" I asked.

"No, but he wants to come see me," she said. "I'm surprised he'd even look my way because he's light skinned and...." She hesitated. "Well, you know how some boys feel about dark-skinned girls," she said. "If you ain't light skinned, then they think you're ugly."

"Yeah," I said, "I know, but there are a lot of dark-skinned girls I see who are pretty. But all they see is dark skin. No features, no curves, just dark skin. Yellow doesn't mean you're pretty and Mom said that if you have nasty ways then you're ugly, no matter what complexion you are. I'm going over to Big Jan's house to see what Emma's been up to," I said. "Talk to you later."

I walked to Big Jan's house and went upstairs. Nobody was there but Emma, a girl I knew only a little named Roselee who lived a few blocks away, and a new face. She was sort of dark-skinned with very little hair for eyebrows. She had a tiny nose and mouth, and her hair was short and pressed. She was thin, but she had curves. She was cute. I looked into her eyes and had this sense that she was hiding something. She had this sad look about her.

"Lawd, look who's back," Emma said. "When you git back?"

"Just now," I said.

Emma and I hugged each other. She was glad to see me and I was glad to see her.

"How you like New York?" she asked.

"I liked it," I said. "It's much bigger than Philly."

"How's your crazy cousin?" she asked.

"Still crazy," I said, laughing. I was feeling a little uncomfortable because I didn't know Roselee that well and I didn't know this other girl at all. Then Emma introduced them to me.

"Nita, this is Roselee and Marlene."

"Hi," I said.

"Hi," they responded.

"Y'all smoke?" I asked.

"Lawd, chald," Emma said. "Don't tell me you smokin'. I know that crazy cousin of yours taught you."

I started to laugh again. Then I lit up another cigarette. "Look at you," she said, as if scolding me.

"Show me?" Roselee asked.

"All you gotta do is take in some smoke and breathe it in backwards," I said. Marlene also wanted to try it, then Emma, who started choking, and we started laughing. She didn't like it so she never tried it again.

"When did she start hanging around here?" I was referring to Roselee.

"Her mom started coming to my house and brought her here with her one day. So ever since then, she's been comin' 'round," Emma said.

I eventually got to know Marlene and Roselee more and more. Roselee was a pretty brown girl. She had medium-length hair that was very thick and a nice body that attracted a lot of guys. She was what we used to call "conceited" in a funny way because every time she had something to say, she would look in the mirror at herself and begin talking.

Marlene began to latch on to me and confide in me about things that were going on in her life. I had known her mom for quite some time. As a matter of fact, everybody knew her. She was what you'd call "common." I was surprised to find out that she had a daughter, but then I found out that Marlene lived with relatives because her mom drank all the time and couldn't take care of her.

She shared a story with me about one of her mom's boyfriends who used to put his mouth on her private parts when her mom was drunk and asleep. I begged her to tell her mother what he was doing to her, but she said that she was scared. I insisted that she tell, so one day she said that she would. Afterwards I didn't see her for awhile, but when I finally did see her again, she told me that her mom went berserk after she told her what he was doing and accused her of lying. She said that her mom made her strip and then she beat her private parts with a leather strap. I was horrified when I heard what she was saying, and at the same time I blamed myself for making her tell. I thought that if anybody would have believed her, it would have been her mom.

After that, we kept secrets. I would cry in bed when I thought about Marlene, but I never let Sharon see me. Marlene was only eleven and shouldn't have been going through this. I wanted to rescue her, but I couldn't. That night I rolled over and reached down into my brown paper bag filled with various brands of cigarette butts I had collected from off the street, lit one up, said a prayer for Marlene, and went to sleep.

Several weeks went by and I was getting ready to go to my first party. I was thirteen. My mom decided to let us go to parties even though she wasn't too fond of the idea, but she said that she used to love to dance when she was young. Besides, she said that she'd rather us tell her where we were going and then give us a set time when we had to be back home rather than us sneaking around. She didn't like that sneaking around stuff. On the other hand, my dad forbade us to go, but he worked at night and never found out. My mom was always more flexible than my father was. We had house parties back then. The parents would go upstairs and as long as everybody agreed not to bring any liquor, we could stay until midnight.

I felt guilty going to a party because I had been baptized. What happened to my commitment to be Christ-like? I felt like a hypocrite, but at the same time I didn't want to feel left out. I wanted to have fun like everybody else.

Reverend Carter came by a couple more Sundays. One time I remember him asking us to come downstairs. My sister and I were hiding upstairs and pretending not to be at home. My mom knew we were up there, but she didn't bother to make us come down, although we could hear them talking. My mom was worried because like I said before, she sent us to Sunday school and church because she believed that it would keep us from sinning. I peeked downstairs at Reverend Carter. When he looked up, I jumped back because I didn't want him to see me. I was ashamed. "Don't worry, Mother, they'll be back. They'll have to come back."

I went to pick up Emma and Roselee at Emma's house. Emma still wasn't ready because she didn't think she looked right in her clothes because she was still flat chested, so we suggested that she stuff herself with lots of toilet paper. For some unknown reason we believed that toilet paper was the answer to your problem if you were still flat chested. After that, we applied make-up to our juvenile features and attached pieces of blonde hair we snipped from Barbie's head to our hair with bobby pins so that it looked like we had blonde streaks. We decided to wear jeans and blouses.

Sharon, Patricia, Cherylanne, and several other girls who lived up the street met us around the front, which was Collom Street. Emma lived around the back. You walked through an alley to get to her house, which was the only house that sat in the back of our houses. The bottom-side girls also were going to the party. We were considered girls from the top-side because we lived close to Germantown Avenue. If you lived behind Germantown Avenue, then you were from the bottom side.

Lots of teenagers came out that night. There hadn't been a party in awhile and when word got around that somebody was having a house party, then nobody stayed at home.

This was where I met William, who was my first love. I was in high school at the time.

We entered the house, which was dark, but the music was already playing. At that moment someone went to screw in a red light bulb. The house quickly filled with boys eager to grab any girl and dance. Fast dancing was easy for me, but I wasn't too comfortable with slow dancing with a boy because that was something I'd never done before. Besides, I had only done the two-step with Debbie when she taught Sharon and I.

I was approached by this guy who wanted to slow dance. I used to see him at the Keystone with the Corner Boys, but he never noticed me. They used to say that he ran my neighborhood, so I knew that he had somewhat of a reputation, but I never paid him any attention because I wasn't into boys. I used to be a tomboy and used to climb barbed wire fences and stone walls with Lonnie, who was one of my best friends. We didn't have any trees to climb, but sometimes we would scale the side of this wall that led you to the top of the roof of this dilapidated garage next to Emma's house and then jump off. Lonnie was more of a tomboy than me. She could do anything most boys could do but pee like one, so boys were the furthest thing from our minds. Another reason why he didn't notice me was because I still wore my hair in platts until Debbie showed me how to do my own hair.

He was cute and he was a good dancer. And when I looked down at his feet, I noticed that he had bow legs. I looked around for Roselee and Emma. By now, we were all paired off and on the dance floor. I looked over at Emma again and noticed this guy squeezing her breasts, so I started laughing. "What's so funny?" William asked.

"Oh, I'm not laughing at you, I was just thinking about something."

He wanted to dance with me again and again and again. He was my dance partner until I decided to leave before midnight hit.

He asked me if he could walk me home. I told him that he could. He wanted to know how old I was, and I told him I was sixteen, even though I was only thirteen, because I felt myself drawn to him. He had a bad-boy reputation and the fact that he was attracted to me was turning me on. He told me that he lived on the next block and that he wanted to call me sometime. We exchanged numbers and then he went through the alley, which was a shortcut to his house.

I was soon joined by Sharon, Patricia, Cherylanne, Emma, and Roselee. The first thing that came out of their mouths was that William liked me. I started blushing, then I told Emma that I saw this guy squeezing her breasts. "He said they were soft," Emma said. Roselee, Emma, and I started laughing because we knew that he was feeling toilet paper.

William and I began to talk on the phone a lot and it wasn't long before my mom found out. I would also soon find out that Ms. Robin lived next door to his house and saw me standing outside his door one day. My mom was upset when she found out. Ms. Robin had already informed her that his mom and dad were alcoholics and that when he was younger, he accidentally knocked his mother's eye out trying to break up a fight between the two of them. I was eavesdropping the day she told my mom and was shocked to hear that had happened, even though I never mentioned it to him.

My mom didn't want me to see him anymore. She was afraid for me and said that I was too young to date. She felt that he was carrying a lot of turmoil within himself and then on top of that, she said he was too old for me. Ms. Robin was the one who informed her that he was eighteen, but that still didn't stop me from seeing him when I would go to the store, which was quite often. Since my mom did hair, someone was always coming back and telling her that they saw us together, so she decided to let him come to my house at a decent time and leave at a decent time. The first day he came to my house my mom told him how old I really was. I was mad and at the same time embarrassed, and I didn't think that he would want to see me anymore since he was five years older than me.

It had just turned dark outside and my mom was going upstairs to lay down. I walked William outside to the porch. "I can't believe a young girl has my nose open," he said. We had a street light in front of our house that spread light halfway across our porch. He leaned up against the banister and took me by the hands, then pulled me to him. I was shy and wouldn't look into his face, so he took his hand and lifted my chin so that I would look into his eyes. His smooth chocolate complexion didn't have any blemishes and his jet black hair and brown eyes were very appealing to me.

He continued to look into my eyes and said they were pretty. Then he asked me to close them and to part my lips. I felt stupid because I didn't know why he was asking me to do such a silly thing, so I started laughing with my eyes still shut. "Now I can tell that you're only thirteen." I was embarrassed again, but he was smiling. His teeth were straight and white.

He asked me again to close my eyes and part my lips. This time I didn't laugh. He put his lips on mine and stuck his tongue in my mouth.

I snapped, "What are you doing?"

"You never heard of a French kiss?" he asked.

"No, what is it?" I asked.

"Are you for real?" he asked again.

"Yeah," I said. I had never heard of a French kiss. Then he asked me to close my eyes and part my lips a third time. He pulled me very close to him and again put his tongue in my mouth, but this time, I felt different. His kiss aroused every part of my body. Then all of a sudden I felt something very hard, so I jumped back. "What's that I feel?"

"I popped a hardy," he said.

"A what?" I asked.

"When a guy gets excited, his thing gets hard," he said. He smiled faintly. I could tell that he was embarrassed, then I felt embarrassed. I was growing up too fast.

At first we could go outside our neighborhood if we wanted to party, which included Dogtown, Pulaski Town, Haines Street, Summerville, North Philly, South Philly, and West Philly. It was no big thing, but some gang members began to become real territorial and didn't want other guys dancing with their girls, so we stayed in our own turf. We began to feel the same way, which caused us to form a strong bond among ourselves. We were the Brickyard girls; they were the Brickyard boys or the Corner Boys, as we sometimes called them because they'd stand on the corner singing doo-wop or a cappella.

I continued to see William, but the more I got to know him the more violent he became. For one, if he thought that I was looking at another guy, he'd slap me across the face, then later apologize and say that he did it because he loved me, and I believed him. In spite of the hits, his kisses were always sweet and his touch always gentle.

He invited me to his house one day when his mom and dad were there, so I would finally get a chance to meet them. I was nervous because I had heard that they were alcoholics. I sneaked through the big alley when my mom was in the kitchen. I knocked on his door lightly so that Ms. Robin wouldn't hear from next door and tell where I was. I was greeted by a woman who appeared to be in her fifties. She had a heavy smell of alcohol on her breath.

"Hello," she said quite pleasantly. "I know you came to see my Billy. Come on in," she said. It was obvious to me that one of her eyes wasn't real because she didn't realize that she had put it in crooked. It startled me at first. Even when she would blink, only one eyelid would close. I could hear someone in the kitchen trying to sing when she said, "That's his father trying to sing. Don't he sound a mess?" She chuckled. All of her teeth were missing. "Go upstairs," she said. "Billy's in his room." But as I approached the steps, his father stumbled out from the kitchen. Neither one of them were too tall. She was about my complexion and he was a shade or two darker. They both had salt-and pepper-colored hair. His hair was short and curly. I could tell that at one time they were an attractive couple, but drinking had taken its toll on them.

He stood there and stared at me. I didn't know what to think, wondering if he was going to start cursing like my dad did when he was drunk, but instead he stuck his index finger in his mouth like a little boy and a sad expression fell over his face. It reminded me of the face of a lonely clown. Then he took his finger from out of his mouth and broke into an almost toothless grin. His mother started to laugh. I felt awkward, so I started to laugh with them.

Bill came running down the steps, and I could see that he was embarrassed. He introduced me to his parents and quickly led me to his bedroom. "I hope they didn't scare you," he said.

"No," I said. "As a matter of fact, your dad is funny. Don't be embarrassed. My dad drinks, too."

He turned on some music and sat next to me on his bed. "I want to make love to you," he said. We kissed. Then he removed his pants and shirt. He had a nice body.

He laid me down on his bed and climbed on top of me. He lifted my skirt and blouse, then started moving his body against mine. I could feel his nature rise. "If you don't want to, I won't make you," he said. I wanted to, but I didn't want to mess up my life. *What if I got pregnant?* I thought. He kissed me tenderly on the lips and then on the neck. We were both very aroused. I continued to fight against doubt and passion, but doubt soon won, so as he began to kiss me again, I resisted.

"I can't," I said. He got up and put his clothes back on. I didn't know exactly what he was feeling, but I knew some of it was disappointment, so I left.

My not wanting to go all the way didn't stop William from wanting to see me. We dated for several months and then I didn't see him for awhile—not even a phone call. I worried about him because at times he was depressed and hung around in bad neighborhoods.

Two weeks later he came by my house and knocked on my door. "Where have you been?" I asked.

"Hanging out in North Philly," he said.

"What have you been doing down there?" I asked.

His eyes were glassy and he acted very strangely. We took a walk down the street. We kissed and then he showed me his arm, which had a long trail of dark spots on it.

"What happened to your arm?" I asked, confused.

"I shoot dope," he said. I laughed because the word *dope* sounded stupid. That word had not yet entered our vocabulary. It's drugs," he said. "It makes me feel good. I got problems and sometimes I can't cope."

I couldn't comprehend what he was talking about. I had never heard of anyone shooting drugs into their arms, let alone just to feel good or to solve their problems.

I didn't see him again for several more weeks and then he called to tell me that he had joined the Marine Corps. I was scared for him. "Why did you do that?" I asked. "So many boys are dying over there in Vietnam."

"It will help me get my life together," he said. "I've been doing a lot of negative things. Give me a chance. If you love me, you'll wait for me."

I didn't know what to say. I just wanted him to get help. We spent the whole day together before he left. I wanted to go to the airport with him, but he left too early in the morning.

Then the letters started coming. I got one every other day. I wasn't good at writing letters, so I got Sharon to write them for me. At one point I stopped writing. I hadn't seen him for a while and because I was so young, I was afraid that I might be losing my feelings for him, but the day he came home, I could see that I still loved this boy.

I met him at his house. He was still dressed in his dress blues. We decided to walk to my house since my family had grown to like him, although I had never shared with any of them about his drug problem which was why he joined the Marines in the first place. He stayed for a couple of hours before he said that he was going to see some of his boys because they didn't know that he was back home. He said that he would be back later on that night, but I didn't see him until the next day. Again his eyes looked glazed. I was afraid of him when I saw him like that. He asked me to take a walk with him through the big alley across from my house next to the Keystone. "I'm leaving for good," he said. "And I won't be coming back."

I didn't know where he was coming from. "What are you talking about?" I asked.

"I want you to find someone else," he said.

"But I don't want any one else. I love you," I said.

"I'm not good enough for you," he said. "I'll never be good enough for you. Besides, when I go to Vietnam, I'll get killed. I want to die at home." He pulled out a small handgun.

"What are you going to do with that thing?" I asked.

"Kill myself," he said.

My heart started racing and then I panicked and started crying. "Please don't do it," I begged him.

"You have to go on without me," he said.

"Give me the gun," I said.

"No," he said. "Go home."

At that point, I was afraid that he might turn the gun on me as well, so I left. I didn't want to, but I couldn't change his mind. As I turned my back to walk away from him, the last words he said to me were, "I'll be dead by the time you get home."

After he spoke those words, I felt like he had just shot me in the heart. I never turned around to see him again.

I went straight to my bedroom without saying a word, just hoping that he really didn't mean what he said, but my heart was telling me something else. I had the feeling that sooner or later the phone would ring and whoever answered it would be telling me that he was dead. I was sick to my stomach.

Not so long afterwards the phone rang.

My sister was hysterical and said that he had been shot. Then I became hysterical. My mom was crying.

Because I was the last person to see him alive, I had to give a police report. It was like reliving the whole thing all over again. I was hating him and loving him at the same time, hating him because he selfishly ended his life and now I was hurting and going through all this trauma by myself. He was depressed and I didn't know why. I didn't know how to help him, but now he was dead, and I was still living, going through this hell.

He was given a military funeral. My mom worried about me for the next few months because I kept mostly to myself and stayed in my room a lot. My mom never wanted me to date at such a young age, but she was afraid that I would somehow see him anyway, and she was right—I would have found a way. On the other hand, my dad was angry that I was allowed to see him in the first place, even though he had grown to like him.

My mom was there for me, and so were my sister and my friends. My mom said that time heals all wounds. I asked her if a girl my age could fall in love, but she said that it was puppy love. Then she said, "You never forget your first love."

Emma left Big Jan's house to come and live in our house because Big Jan kept bad company. Emma would have money, and people were saying that Big Jan's male friends were taking advantage of her, but like I said before, we learned how to keep secrets. My mom always held a special place in her heart for Emma and welcomed her into our home and so she grew up in our house as one of our sisters.

Gang warfare had taken on a whole new twist. It got to the point where you weren't even safe in school or after school anymore. Teeney was from Haines Street. She was about five-foot-four and very thin, with a dark complexion. Her skin was rough like her spirit. She had a tooth missing in the front of her mouth and she always wore a bandana tied around her permed hair. She would fight you for no reason at all. She was small in stature, but as strong as she was mean. I felt sorry for any girl who was her next victim. When she'd walk the streets, her boys followed behind her. She was feared throughout the entire school.

I heard rumors one day that she was going to fight this girl after school. I asked several people I knew, "What for?" and nobody knew why. What it boiled down to was that if she didn't like you, then she would lay in the cut after school and attack her prey like a fierce mountain lion on a prowl. I felt sorry for this girl. I used to see her quite often. She was quiet and kept to herself. She was also attractive and I believe that's why Teeney wanted to fight her.

As she walked home from school, Teeney was walking behind her with half the school behind her. They were instigating because everybody wanted to see a fight, especially the boys if it was two girls involved because once they tore each other's clothes off, they could see some titties. This girl was overcome with fear, but she continued to walk home as she carried her books under her arms, never looking back at Teeney who was now shouting profane words at the girl. All of a sudden she leaped on her while she commenced to whipping her. Then she picked her up and hurled her through a glass storefront window.

I didn't stick around to see what happened after that because I didn't like Teeney. We used to say that she had the devil in her and that's why she was so strong and so mean.

We decided to go up Haines Street one day to visit our aunt, being careful not to run into any girls from that turf. The good thing was that our aunt lived at the beginning of Haines Street, therefore we didn't have to walk deep into the neighborhood to see her. If we did, we would have gotten our asses whipped by the Haines Street girls, which was also Teeney's turf.

We only stayed a little while because it wouldn't be safe if we left too late. My aunt was the type who knew everybody and knew who everybody was related to. Before we left, we saw Teeney coming down the street on the opposite side from where my aunt lived, and she called her to come over. "This is your cousin," she said. We just stood there with our mouths open until she said "hi." We became close with her after that, and the more we got to know her, the crazier we knew she was.

After school we remained in our own turf, including on the weekends. We looked forward to the weekends because we would put our money together from little part-time jobs and buy beer, liquor and cigarettes.

Our favorite place to hang out was in the big alley which led to Big Jan's house. We would sit on milk crates and sing do-wop a cappella. The boys crooned on the corner and we crooned in the alley. And when we went in the house, Mom was still doing hair while the news was on and then we'd hear, "Another black boy was shot and killed due to gang violence." Martin Luther King was fighting for our civil rights and we were fighting and killing one another.

Sharon was in New York visiting my brother. She would be attending college and was contemplating going to a school out there. Roselee and I boarded the train to go meet her. We would be staying for a couple of days and then we all would be coming back to Philadelphia together. Roselee was excited because she had never been to New York. We only needed about twelve dollars, and the ride only took about three hours. We were both looking out the window as the train slowed down near our destination. As the train was beginning to stop, our eyes beheld the most beautiful sight—a beautiful brown sister with a woolen crown that covered her entire head walked proudly amongst the masses of people. As the train slowed down, we continued to follow her with our eyes. By the time we stepped off the train, she had slipped into the crowd. As soon as we saw Sharon, all we could talk about was this girl's hair as we tried to describe what we had just seen. "This girl had her hair combed out, only it wasn't straightened or permed," we said. "I mean, it was just full and round."

Sharon said, "Oh, they wear that down here. It's called a 'freedom'."

Roselee asked, "What does that mean?"

Then Sharon said, "Freedom means freedom from the straightening comb and perm."

Roselee and I had decided to wear a freedom just as soon as we got back to Philly. Sharon also informed us that some people called them "naturals" or "afros." Afro would eventually be the word most commonly used. Roselee and I were trend setters. We set the trend at our school for mini-skirts, maxi-shirts, rope-net stockings, fish-net stockings, micro-minis and square-toed shoes. We dared to be different because we liked it.

We got back that Sunday, and that Monday morning I got up early and asked my mom if she would please wash my hair. I hadn't yet told her what I had planned on doing because I didn't know what her response would be. She might think that I was crazy for wanting to wear nappy hair to school. "I won't have time to do anything to it," she said. "You might be late for school."

"I don't want it done," I said. "I'm going to dry it and wear it like it is." I was curious to hear what she was going to say.

"I don't understand," she said. "You mean just like that?"

"Yeah," I said. "They wear it like that in New York."

Sharon came in the shop and asked, "Are you really wearing your hair like that?"

"Yeah!" I said. "I'm really wearing my hair natural."

My mom washed it and dried it and then combed it out. I called Roselee and asked her if she was still wearing her hair in a freedom. She said that she had already washed it and was on her way over. We wore mini-skirts and afros.

All eyes were on us as we walked like proud peacocks up Germantown Avenue. When we got to school, people were still staring. One girl asked, "How did you get your hair like that?" We responded in unison, "Wash it!"

Then others began to ask the same question and we continued to give them the same simple answer: "Wash it!"

The next day a couple more girls started wearing their hair natural. The next thing we knew the fellas took that Congolene out of their heads and started wearing an afro, even little children and grandmothers began wearing afros.

We took pride in wearing our hair natural, but we still continued to fight one another. Often when mom turned on the television, we'd hear how another black boy died from gang violence. We continued to hang out with Teeney, although Emma and Sharon never did. Emma was doing good in school and Sharon was soon to graduate. Cherylanne and Patricia went to Catholic school and me, I just didn't give a damn. I had someone new to hang out with at school. We thought alike, we had the same name, we were both left-handed, and we shared the same zodiac sign. She was short and stacked with a mouth that always got her into trouble, but she didn't need any back-up because she was her own back-up. She *was* Brickyard. We had developed a bad reputation at school and were out of school more than we were in school. Girls began to fear us because they associated us with Teeney. I remember one day standing on the school grounds looking in my school bag for something when I overheard this girl saying, "Don't ever say anything to her. She's crazy." I looked over to see who they were talking about, and they were looking at me! They quickly turned their heads and walked away, but I felt proud because for the first time I remember feeling like somebody. I wasn't noticed in the sixth grade. I was a gamma, stupid, in the dumb group. Now I was getting attention, but I wasn't aware that it was the wrong kind of attention that I was getting. I felt that if I wasn't going to get attention for not being smart, then I was going to get attention for being crazy.

Tammy Watson was from my turf. She had become close to Teeney, but I was closer to Tammy. The more Teeney and Tammy were together, the more Teeney's boyfriend seemed to like Tammy. I used to tell her to watch out for Teeney because I didn't trust her, but she wouldn't listen. Then one day Tammy didn't come to school. We hookied that day as usual and Teeney, her boyfriend, and some other girls from her turf met at a restaurant on Germantown Avenue. Teeney had that evil look in her eyes like the mountain lion waiting for its prey. She began to plot on how she was going to lure Tammy to an isolated place and then stab her in the back. I went back and told Tammy what she had planned on doing. She was hurt, but I had warned her about Teeney. I stopped being with Teeney after that. Tammy came to school one more time and then she stopped. She suffered from depression anyway, and when she was in school, she slept in the back of the classroom all the time.

The civil rights movement had intensified, the white man was "the devil." Malcolm's spirit was still saying, "By any means necessary," Stockley said, "If they don't give to us, then we're going to kick the leg from under the table and take it." James Brown was saying, "I'm black and I'm proud." Nina Simone was the beautiful black woman. Dark skin and full lips were in, and through the civil rights experience, the black student union was created. They were young, they were black, and they were proud. They wanted a more rounded view of black history. It was the black student union in Philadelphia who planned the first walkout, organized by the late David P. Richardson, to protest the negligence on the part of a racist school board.

We were already in bed the night before the walkout. That was when I first heard of it. Sharon said that the black student union had organized a walkout at 10 A.M. I had attended only one student meeting, because I was too busy trying to be a hoodlum. Sharon may have attended more. She said that they would be walking from Germantown High School all the way to City Hall. I rolled over to look at her. "So are you really gonna walk out?"

"Yeah," she said. "I'll be in the auditorium at the time. If you're in class, just walk out," she said.

I had butterflies from the time I got up until the time I got to school. Once I sat down in the classroom, I couldn't keep my eyes off of the clock. Then I got to thinking, *What if I'm the only one who stands up at ten o'clock and walks out?* That made me even more tense. The seconds were ticking. I'd look at the teacher and then at the second hand until the clock struck ten.

I didn't have to wonder any longer. One by one, students slammed their books on the desk and walked out. Germantown High School was predominately black, so the only kids left in my classroom were four white girls. I went to the auditorium and met Sharon where she told me she would be waiting. I told her about the events as they had unfolded in our classroom and then she told me what had happened in the auditorium at ten o'clock.

"The teacher was up on the stage reading the morning announcements," she said. "Nobody was paying any attention to what she was saying except for the few white kids who were asking questions. Everybody else was tense and restless, and they all had their eyes on the clock, but when ten o'clock struck, nobody moved. They just looked at each other. Everybody seemed to have had the same thought in mind which was, *I don't want to be the first one to stand up.* Then all of a sudden, this girl stood up, looked over the balcony, and yelled, 'Ya'll know what time it is! Get up!' Everybody jumped to their feet and walked out."

We headed down Germantown Avenue. We marched in hundreds at first, but when we would approach another high school, the students came to the windows to see what the commotion was. Then someone would yell up to the windows and tell them what we were doing. "Come on down and march with us," we shouted. Without hesitation, they came out and joined us. We continued to do this until our numbers had now reached into the thousands, which included gang members as well. It was the first time gang members would unify. And it was the first time a seed had been planted in me. Would this be the turning point in gang activity? Only time would tell.

City Hall was but a cloudy figure, but we persevered and the more we did, the more fired up we became. City Hall was close to the school board building, but when you walk south down Broad Street, City Hall is the only blurred image that you see. We continued to walk and the cloudy figure became more and more clear. Once we were there, we ran to the school board building. The police were already waiting with riot paraphernalia. I was sort of in the middle of the crowd and could see them beating students with their billy clubs. The keynote speaker began shouting on his bullhorn screaming for them to stop. He said that we hadn't come to riot and we were unarmed. We had come in peace to voice our concerns to the school board and exercise freedom of speech.

After he said that, they seemed to back off. He continued to voice our demands before a cheering crowd of students. Then he began to charge the police force with inappropriate conduct and police brutality. We began to shout, "Police brutality!" before an angry mob of cops.

After the demonstration was over, we hitched rides and rode back home. I thought that my mom would be mad at us, but she supported the whole thing. Later on that night, we turned on the television, and our march had made international news. What we didn't know was that Rizzo, who was the police chief at that time, had sent police in riot gear to every subway stop to attack the students.

The march was only partly successful. Black History still isn't a required subject, but we are learning more about the great contributions of our ancestors and those of us who descend from them. However Black History month was created through that walkout.

Gang activity had ceased but for a season, and once again it was resurrected. One year had passed. We were listening to the radio the day Martin Luther King was shot. We left the radio on the porch and ran in the house. Mom had a customer that day, so she had not yet heard. Sometimes she listened to the radio or looked at the television while she did hair and sometimes she didn't. "Martin Luther King got shot," we all said. "Turn on the television. We just heard it on the radio."

"Is he dead?" she asked reluctantly.

"We don't know," we said, "but they said that he had just been shot in the head." (Even though later we would find out that he was shot in the neck.) When we turned on the television, it was already breaking news. Martin Luther King was lying on this platform, and Jesse Jackson was pointing his finger as if he was showing which direction the bullet had come from. By this time Mom had stopped curling her customer's hair and we were all glued to the television set. "He's not going to make it," she said somberly.

"Why do you say that, Mom?" I asked nervously. I believed everything my mom said, but this time I didn't want to believe her. I didn't want Martin Luther King to die. We continued to watch the events unfold until he was finally pronounced dead. We all knew that somebody white would be responsible for the shooting because whites feared him.

I looked at my mom and then at her customer. Tears were running down their faces. I watched as she struggled to finish her hair. They kept showing the shooting over and over again on every major station in the city. That night we heard a commotion outside. I went outside to the porch. People were running up toward Germantown Avenue, some of whom looked over at me as I stood on the porch. "Come on," they said. "Follow us. It's our turn to get even. We're going to break into their stores and take what we want." I knew what they were talking about—they were going out looting. Somebody was running behind them and said, "No, stop! That's not what Dr. King would have wanted us to do." But they kept on running. I wanted to do what Dr. King would have done, but I was angry, too. I wondered whether I should stay or go, then I saw some empty whiskey bottles that hadn't been broken yet. They were just lying there in the alley across the street from my house next to the Keystone. They looked as if they were saying, "What are you waiting for? Pick us up and throw us as hard as you can!"

I started throwing them against the Keystone wall. It was the only way I could let out my anger. Sharon saw me breaking the bottles, so she ran over and started breaking bottles too. Then I just let out a loud scream. As the days followed, we wondered what direction black people would take. I felt scared and insecure. Martin Luther King was supposed to stop the lynchings and the hatred. He preached nonviolence, but it was violence that took his life. We were now like sheep without a shepherd.

And even though Martin Luther King was dead, we continued to kill one another.

I don't know how far back gang activity goes, but my brother said that when he was my age, there was still a gang called the Brickyard, although the Brickyard itself was divided into three sections: the top-side, the bottom-side, and the tender-line. Everybody from the bottom-side hung around the top-side of Collom Street located near Germantown Avenue. They either stood on the corner or somewhere around the Keystone. The tender-line was an area between the top-side and the bottom-side of the Brickyard. People who lived there somehow escaped the violence that we lived with every day. Our rivals were Haines Street, Dogtown, Pulaski Town, and Summerville, also known as the Ville. The Ville had become increasingly vicious. There was a popular song out called, "Don't Mess with Bill," by the Marvalettes, and they changed the name to "Don't Mess with the Ville."

The year was 1969. Thirty-one black boys in Philadelphia were killed in gang activity. This type of gang activity only encouraged us to become more violent and more determined to protect our turf and keep outsiders from coming in. There was a time we'd witness someone from our turf fight another gang member with their fists, or we'd break an antenna from someone's car and chase them out of our neighborhood or we'd find a stick or a bottle or brick or something to throw at them while we ran them from our turf, but now guns were easier to get our hands on and it was easier to shoot your victim rather than chase him down. It became more satisfying. If you killed someone from another gang, then your gang looked and felt more powerful. One of our gang members made the terrible mistake of going to a party one night outside his territory. But before that would happen, one day he had this heavenly experience with God. He had stopped gangwaring and use to preach to everybody about Jesus and going to church until the Corner Boys started to avoid him. They used to call him the "Apostle." He got tired of being ostracized by his homeboys and made a decision to gangwar again. They went to a party up on Haines Street, and he was gunned down as he tried to get back to his turf. He called to his homeboys and to his brother, who were already several feet in front of him and running for their own lives, to help him as he lay in the streets dying with six bullets in his chest, but at that point it would have been impossible for them to help him because they were all outnumbered and would have been killed just like him.

 The next day I remember this girl running up Germantown Avenue with the Corner Boys to retaliate against Haines Street. She had her two babies with her, running and pushing them in their babycoach. She was just fifteen. She used to say with pride that her second child was Brickyard's baby because they all had her. She was running that day to help defend her baby's daddies.

 Something had to be done about gang activity if we were going to survive as a race of people. All of our young black men were dying. I was riding the twenty-three trolley down Germantown Avenue one day when I heard a loud noise coming from somewhere. I looked out the window and saw this van with a coffin on top of it. The lid to the coffin appeared to be open, and a body was lying inside. It blew my mind when I first saw it. It startled me because I thought that the body inside was real. I began to listen to what the person behind the wheel was saying, but I only heard a part of it because the trolley started moving again. He was the Reverend Melvin Floyd. Reverend Floyd had started his own campaign and ministry to wipe out gang violence once and for all. He would use a dummy to demonstrate to young people how they would end up if they kept fighting one another. He would also hold meetings at various churches and show re-enactments of stories depicting black boys killing one another senselessly over territory they claimed as their own, but in reality still belonged to the white man.

I took a flier from my door one day which read that he would be airing one of these movies at one of the churches in our neighborhood. I asked Sharon and Emma if they would go with me because I wanted to see what he had to say. Emma decided to go, but Sharon refused. She was a gang member to the end and wasn't about to change. She said that Reverend Floyd was just trying to get more members for his church. Cherylanne and Patricia felt the same way. Anita was nowhere to be found, so we went without her. The meeting was supposed to start at eight, but it started once every seat was filled and everybody had quieted down. I was surprised to see so many people, but then someone told me that he had actually used gang members from each neighborhood to do the re-enactment, so a lot of people had showed up just to see themselves on the movie screen. When the skit was over, Reverend Floyd put in another film, only this would be the real thing. The film took you inside the morgue where actual footage of young black boys were shown on metal tables, naked, their bodies riddled with bullet holes. Then came the autopsy. People started throwing up and saying, "Eeeel." Others left. In conclusion, he said in plain and simple words, "You could be next."

I thought about those words all night long with images that were very graphic. I also shared with Sharon what I had just experienced. She wasn't there to witness what I had seen, but she was affected by what I was telling her. "Leave the gang," I said. "It's not worth it."

That night, she declared herself no longer a member of the Brickyard gang. We got some rift from the Corner Boys, but we didn't care. Reverend Floyd saved our lives. Not so long after that, we started a club called T.W.S., which stood for "Together We Stand."

Groups began springing up in various parts of the city to combat gang activity. One group I remember in particular was the Young Black Alliance. They were an all-male group from North Philadelphia, one of the cities hit hardest by gang activity. We were an all-female group. They used to hold socials which consisted of two gangs from a different turf. We decided to hold a meeting between the groups to seek and receive suggestions on how we could bring our gang and their gang together. Would these socials create a carefully woven fabric of young people all over the city, and would these young people work together to keep this carefully woven fabric intact? Well, that was the goal. It looked as though we were finally pulling ourselves up by our own boot straps. It would at least be a start.

The weekend of the meeting, we boarded the twenty-three trolley and headed down to North Philly. We were scared. I'd never been down to North Philly because their gangs were some of the toughest in Philadelphia. But we had to start somewhere.

The streets were somewhat bare because we held the meeting on a Sunday, which took place upstairs over an empty storefront. The building was well maintained and very clean, although it was also very drafty. Chairs were scattered about as if a previous meeting had already taken place, so we re-arranged them and sat down. We had heard that Sammy Davis Jr. wanted to do something to help the cause, so during the meeting we made plans to contact him.

When the meeting was over and it was time to go, we looked up at the door that had a glass window and saw the angry faces of North Philadelphia girls eyeing us up and down or "grittin,'" as we called it. At that moment, we didn't think that we would leave North Philly alive. I also thought that going to that meeting was the biggest mistake we had made, but the leader of the Young Black Alliance stepped outside the door and said something to them. We knew they felt intimidated by us and thought that we came to move in on their turf, which included their homeboys, because they were still living out their days of ignorance. He then entered the room and told us that it was safe to leave. Apparently they respected him, and on top of that he was extremely good looking. He seemed to have had his homegirls in check, because they escorted us to the trolley stop and we made it home in one piece.

Sharon and Emma helped organize the Sammy Davis Jr. event. I couldn't make it because I had somewhere else to be. It was called "A Night to Remember." Mr. Davis gave of himself unselfishly before a sell-out crowd in North Philadelphia and for the first time in a long time, it was safe to enter someone else's turf.

There was a girl in my classroom in high school who used to wear long skirts all the time and a head covering that resembled close to what nuns wear on their heads. She was always very quiet and kept to herself. We had a couple of classes together and because she had this peaceful vibe about her, I always chose to sit next to her. I was impressed by her mannerisms. She seemed to have a discipline that I didn't have because everything she did seemed to be in complete order and harmony. I asked her one day why she wore long skirts and dresses, and she told me that she was a black Muslim, which meant that she followed the teachings of the honorable Elijah Muhammad.

"What are some of the things y'all do?" I asked.

She said, "Well, we have to attend meetings at the temple and the minister gives a speech on how we should conduct ourselves in our daily lives. He teaches us the truth about the white man, who is the devil."

"The white man is the devil?" I asked. "Why do y'all believe that?"

"Because of all of the evil things that they have done to us as a race of people," she said. "We don't eat pork because the pig is an unclean animal," she continued.

"What do you mean by that?" I asked.

"It contains a worm that will get inside you and make you ill," she said. "We don't want to dress like white women because they disgrace themselves by wearing short skirts and dresses, showing their behinds, and we cover our hair because it is every woman's beauty," she explained.

I was impressed by what she said since it sounded so right. She invited me to the temple and even offered to give me some of her skirts so that I wouldn't have any excuses not to go. My mom taught me how to sew, so I eventually started making my own clothes. This was a major turning point in my life that would change the way I looked and felt about myself. The Nation of Islam empowered black people by offering them hope for the first time, along with self-respect, self-reliance, love for oneself, discipline, and a sense of pride and dignity. I tried to get my mom to stop eating pork because she suffered from high blood pressure, but she continued to eat it. I even tried to stop Sharon from eating it, but she didn't stop either, although Emma did.

Time would pass. I had finally graduated, but only by the skin of my teeth. I had one C and the rest were Fs, but I knew people who graduated with me who only read at a first grade level.

I couldn't remember the last time we had organized a block clean-up. I stood on my porch, frustrated because I didn't have a job because jobs were scarce and they didn't pay much if you had one. There was no place to go, no rec centers in the 'hood to keep the youth off of the streets. The Corner Boys were still standing on the corners or drinking beer in the alley or sitting at the Keystone. Sharon and Emma eventually came outside, too, when Sharon saw me staring into space. "What are you thinking about?" she asked.

"You know, something feels strange, but I can't put my finger on it," I said.

I don't know how she made the connection, but she said, "That's because there's no more gangs." She was right. It had been almost a year and I was just realizing it. It was like all the gangs in Philadelphia had called for a cease-fire one day and I never saw the white flag go up. It felt like all of a sudden someone called an end to the Vietnam war. I sat down on the steps and smiled as I began to savor the sweet smell of peace and calm in Philadelphia, but then I thought, *But is this it?* Black neighborhoods were still struggling to stay afloat. Jobs were scarce. Young black people didn't have anywhere to go. We still didn't have the same opportunities as whites.

I stopped going to the mosque. A lot of black people liked the Nation because they taught black men to love one another and to respect their woman, but not all black people believed that all white people or any one white person was a devil—me included. Some of their friends were white or their co-workers or a church member was white. To me this sort of teaching divided those who would accept this teaching from those who didn't and when you have such disputes, then what you are trying to accomplish won't work. That's why I never knew much about the Nation when Malcolm was still alive. No one in my house did, except what we learned through the media.

When I was little, we were taught through the media that Malcolm was a troublemaker and that black people were going to suffer because of him. Whenever I heard his name, I shook. I believed that if he kept saying that the white man was the devil, he was going to have all of us lynched. The media portrayed Malcolm and Martin as opposites and black people believed it, so as you can see, there was a division right there. This kept a lot of black people from joining the Nation or even supporting it. Before Malcolm was assassinated he had stopped calling the white man the devil, but the Nation continued to believe this concept.

Even though I had stopped eating pork, I continued to drink beer and smoke. I finally got a job at a candy factory and was able to buy clothes, beer, and smoke cigarettes. I tried my best to hide my cigarette habit, but one day out of the blue my mom said, "I know y'all smoke." It bothered her, and so it bothered me. She never knew I drank though, until one of the Corner Boys along with Emma and Sharon carried me home because I was too sick and too drunk to walk. I remember staring at my mom because I didn't know who she was. She had tears in her eyes. Then I just started throwing up. I had disgraced myself and disrespected my mom. It was the last time I ever took a drink.

My mom was growing tired of the neighborhood. She had contacted a realtor to help her find another house in Philadelphia in a section called Mount Airy. Mount Airy was where blacks who had a little money lived and where the "lighty bright girls" lived, as we called them, because they were light-skinned. We didn't want any parts of that world. We were upset when Mom told us of her plans to move there. She had been here for many years and had grown tired, but we just didn't understand. We felt that she was being unfair because she was taking us away from our friends and the only life we knew.

One night we went to bed and were awakened by a noise outside our window. I got up to see what it was, then called Sharon and Emma to the window. There was this hazy cloud that encircled the Keystone. "What are they doin'?" I asked, still half asleep. At first we couldn't see anyone, but we could still hear a commotion, and then the haze disappeared. It was then that we saw this guy who was very well dressed walking down the steps of the Keystone and this other guy with a needle still stuck in his arm. It appeared as though the one who gave him the drugs was the one walking away. We saw death that night, and that's why that hazy cloud engulfed the Keystone. It was a strange sight.

I doubled over and fell to my knees. We never saw anybody shoot dope before. We started to cry. The next day, people were talking in the street and said that he had overdosed, and it wasn't too long after that dope spread through my neighborhood like an epidemic. One problem just kinda went out the back door and another one came through the window like a thief in the night. We got rid of the gang problem, but now we were facing a drug problem. We were killing ourselves all over again. The first time was with a bullet, and now it was with a hypodermic needle. People would actually approach you and try to convince you to shoot heroin. They made it sound good, but I kept telling them, "No!" For one, I wasn't giving myself any needle and neither was anybody else, plus I saw how it made William act. He ended up taking his own life. I had a bad vibe about drugs from the beginning and didn't want any parts of it. I wasn't trying to LIVE that way or DIE that way!

Patricia had a friend who wanted her to deliver a bag of something to someone he knew. He gave her directions on how to get there, and she asked us to walk with her. When we got to the apartment, this cute guy was sitting back on a couch. We had never opened the bag and didn't know of its contents until we got there. Inside were small plastic bags filled with leaves. He opened up one of the bags and rolled up a cigarette like Nadine used to do. He told us that it was reefer and offered us one, which we smoked as he told us, "Now you know where to buy a nickel bag." So now we smoked reefer and cigarettes. I still didn't drink, but then one day I decided that I didn't want to smoke reefer or cigarettes anymore. I didn't go any further with it, and I cut loose everybody who continued to do drugs.

Sharon went to the Avenue one day to shop. I didn't feel up to walking, so I waited on the porch for her to come back. When she did come back, she had a newspaper under her arm and a shopping bag in her hand. "What you got there, Muhammad Speaks?" I asked.

"No," she replied. "This is a Black Panther newspaper. These two brothers on Germantown Avenue were selling them.

They wear these black leather jackets. I got a chance to talk to them for awhile," she explained.

She sat her bag down on the porch as Emma was walking out the front door. The man on the front of the paper had our attention because he was fine. The caption under the paper read, "A panther is an animal who is not vicious by nature, but will attack if backed into a corner." Then it went on to say that the Panthers were not violent but would defend themselves if they were provoked. We read the entire paper until we finished it.

We'd had always heard about police brutality in Los Angeles, beginning with the Los Angeles riots, but nothing like that was happening here in Philadelphia, or was it just a well-kept secret that kept us blinded all these years? But then we got to thinking about the gang activity that for so long plagued our neighborhoods. Was it by design, to keep us killing one another? No one tried to stop it, and when a black boy lay dying in the street the cops always took their good ol' time arriving at the scene so that by that time they got there, the boy had already bled to death. The rise of the Black Panther party only confirmed our suspicions, for it was at that time, after the deaths of Malcolm and Martin, that all of the accusations that were made against a racist police force in other cities across America became a reality in Philadelphia, too. The message of the Black Panther Party was spreading and people were beginning to become aware of the violent nature of the Philadelphia police force, headed by Police Chief "Pig" Frank Rizzo, as we called him.

At one time when patrol cars were all red, we had the utmost respect for the police. Whatever they did we said, "Well, they're just doing their job." We used to call them "the man." Now we were calling them "pigs." We continued to read the papers until one day some guy we knew from the West Side took notice as he approached our porch. "That's a Panther newspaper y'all got, ain't it?"

"Yeah," we said, "how you know?"

"Because their headquarters is just down the street from where I live. Why don't y'all come to one of their meetings?

They're all right," he said. He told us that the Black Panthers started a free breakfast program in his neighborhood for the little kids. They believed that a child could perform better in school if he or she had a hot meal in their stomach. Many children in the inner cities would actually go to school hungry every morning. (What no one expected was that the free breakfast program, which was started by the Black Panthers, would one day carry over into the entire school system throughout America.) "Come on," he said. "I'll walk y'all over there." I got an instant rush. I had always wanted to go to a Panther meeting but didn't know where one was. I knew I had to ask my mom if I could go, but I was scared she would say no. The minute I mentioned their name, she cut me off and said, "You stay away from them. Those people are militant. I've heard things in the news about them."

So we pretended to be going to the store and went anyway. The Panthers came with a new message: "The power belongs to the people."

They used the constitution to defend their right to bear arms and to fight against an unjust system that wasn't working for the oppressed people of America, beginning with black people. They weren't evil, but the media wanted it to appear that way because they feared them.

Their headquarters was an old storefront on Pulaski Avenue. We entered the front door into the office of the building. We were then greeted by a brother sitting at a desk. He said, "Power to the people! Did you come here to learn about the Panthers?"

"Yeah," we said. He told us to go into the next room, which was to the left of the office, and find a seat around the table. We went in and found a seat. I was shy, so I sat looking down until I felt comfortable. The brother who sat at the head of the table called on another brother to stand up and recite the ten-point platform. We were told in time that everybody had to learn it and if you were picked to recite it that day, you had better know it or do however many push-ups you were told to do as a form of discipline. He didn't know it, so he had to do fifty. Someone kept eyeing me every time I looked up, then he smiled. His name was Frank, and he was buff. I liked that. He sported a short afro and had pretty brown skin and light brown eyes. He was the one who sold my sister her first paper. After the meeting, he asked me for my name. After we exchanged names, he asked me if he could call me sometimes. I said it was okay. In time, I became his girl.

Once we got back home, Sharon and I told Emma, Patricia, Roselee, Marlene, and Anita about the meeting. We also informed them that the meetings were held at five o'clock every day. Patricia liked the Panthers but she never came to the meetings. Emma couldn't come because she was still in school and always had lots of homework. Roselee wasn't at all interested, but Anita and Marlene were. We went to the meetings every day along with Sharon until we decided to join the organization in 1971. We had to submit an application along with a black and white passport photo we had taken at Woolworth's. Emma joined too, even though she still couldn't attend the meetings, but we kept her well informed. Going to a Panther meeting excited me the way it did when we would meet with Reverend Carter during my church days.

Panther attire was black leather jackets, black berets, and pants if you were a brotha, or pants or skirts for the sistas. If you didn't have a leather jacket, then we were allowed to wear army jackets. Frank had jackets from when he was in Vietnam that he gave to Sharon and me.

Wednesday was our favorite day to be at a Panther meeting because we got to sing songs about the revolution as we marched during drill practice. One song I loved in particular was "Power to the People." The words went like this:

> Power, power to the people
> It's the people's power
> Gun totin' power

> Fred Hampton was a dedicated leader
> Of the Black Panther Party
> He was shot in the head
> For something he said
> He loved the people
> He served the people
> Power, power to the people

I was proud of myself when I finally learned the ten-point platform. Eventually my dad started to see Panther paraphernalia at various places in the house, and he noticed slogans we were using like "right on," "power to the people," and "free Huey." We tried not to use Panther terms when he was in our presence, but they had become so much a part of our everyday language we could no longer help it. He used to tell us that the Panthers were communists and if we were to ever join them that the government would always be watching us and making sure we would never get a job. I pondered over what he said, but as far as we were concerned, that would never happen because we were going to be the new government, and then everybody would have a job. I was a Panther and I was going to die a Panther if I had to, just like little Bobby Hutton and the rest of my comrades.

We never told either of our parents that we had joined the ranks of the Black Panther Party, although my mom suspected that we were going to meetings. However like a lot of parents, they began to support the Panthers because of the free breakfast programs and because they didn't believe that the Panthers were violent like the media portrayed them to be. Then one night our headquarters was raided by Philly's so-called "finest" in a hail of gunfire for one reason only, and that was to make a public example out of the Panthers. "Don't fuck with us," is what they meant! The men were forced to come out before the neighborhood, buck naked in front of the whole community, children included. We had planned on sneaking out that night for a late meeting but had changed our minds because we were too tired, so we read the headlines the next day. At that point, we were ready to challenge any cop who crossed our path. If we saw a cop patrolling our neighborhood, we ran up to the car window and challenged them. We cursed them as they slowed down in their cars scoffing at us. They didn't take us seriously because we were just a small group of young teenage girls. Once their cruiser came to a stop, they'd look us up and down as if to say, "What are y'all gonna do?" Then they would laugh at us and proceed on down the street.

The Panthers were at the height of their reign. Another group who followed a similar platform like the Panthers was the Young Lords, who were a group of Puerto Ricans from the inner cities, too. They also had concerns about equal housing, racism, unemployment, and police brutality in the Spanish community. In Jamaica, Bob Marley had his struggle, and in Africa, Nelson Mandella had his struggle.

You could hardly find a soul in the streets the day Huey P. Newton came to Philadelphia to Mogonical Hall. The twenty-three trolleys were packed like sardines. I didn't wait for anyone because space would have been limited and if I didn't see him that day, then most likely I would have never had an opportunity to see him again. I hopped on an already packed trolley and headed down to Mogonical Hall. There were already masses of people there and still more people arriving every second. I was somewhat near the end of the line when they started letting people in. I grew more and more tense because soon there would be no more room for anybody to get in, but I was lucky that day—I was the last person who would get into Mogonical Hall to see Huey P. Newton. It was impossible to get near him since he was surrounded entirely by bodyguards ready to take a bullet if anyone attempted an assassination. Every now and then when he would move around while making his speech and I would get a glimpse of his beret, but that was it. Yet that didn't prevent any one of us from hearing a dynamic speech that day.

Frank and I had been dating for about two months. Time went by, and then came the rumors and conflicting information about a rift between Huey and Eldrige Cleaver. The biggest rumor was that Huey was living in a luxurious penthouse off of the funds generated through donations and sales of the Black Panther newspapers. We were all shaken by this hearsay, but at a meeting we were told not to believe it, that it was all media hype, a way to destroy the Panther Party. Attack the head and you've destroyed the body. However Frank still became restless and disillusioned. One night after a meeting, he said that he was leaving the Party. I was devastated. After all, he had been responsible for bringing a lot of people into the party, including all of us. "You're not going to be a Panther anymore?" I asked.

"No," he said. "But I'll always be a part of the struggle. I sell newspapers all day, but I'm not making any money. Look, he said, I got out of Vietnam a year and a half ago, and what do I have to show for it? I want more out of life than this. I want to get a good job, get married, and maybe travel, have a couple kids."

I didn't know what to say. I liked him a lot, but if I left too, then I would feel like I was turning my back on the struggle. There was so much work to be done. How could I leave the Panthers and still be a part of the struggle?

That night, he walked me home. After he left, I had a talk with Sharon and I told her that I wasn't going to be a Panther anymore. She looked at me as if I had just stabbed her in the chest. "Why are you leaving?" she asked.

"Because Frank left," I said. "He wants to get a good job and get married one day."

"Ahh, so you're following him?" she said.

"Yeah, but I'm always going to be a revolutionist," I said defensively.

"Yeah, maybe," she said sarcastically.

She went to a couple more meetings with Anita and Marelene, then she stopped going too. She was in a bad relationship which was taking its toll on her.

The Panther empire looked like it was starting to crumble. Vietnam was still very much a part of us. I couldn't stand to hear the news anymore because it was making me sick to my stomach. At times I was depressed, and so was my mom. She had found a cute little house in Mount Airy and since the real estate agent was a friend of the family, he said that he would make it easy for her to get the house with every little money. We still didn't want to move, but it would be her decision. But then instead of going through with the original plan, the realtor went behind her back and signed a contract with another family after jacking up the price on them, even though they were willing to pay the price and could afford it at that. We were glad that we weren't moving, but my mom was sad, although we couldn't comprehend the debt of her pain and she stopped taking her medicine.

Our neighborhood had become a breeding ground for nothing but destruction. Drug dealers now ruled, but we vowed that we would somehow take it back.

Frank came by one night and we decided to take a slow walk down Germantown Avenue. When we got back, I knocked on the door. My mom always answered the door because she was always home, and if she was doing hair, then whichever one of us was there would answer it, so I knocked again, but still no answer. I became worried, then I started thinking crazy stuff like some junkie had broke in and murdered my family. I became hysterical and started banging on the door. "Hold up," Frank said. "I see somebody coming down the steps."

"Where's Mom?" I asked anxiously. "I've been banging on the door for the last few minutes," I said.

"I don't know," Sharon replied. " I just got out of the bathtub. She's probably in the kitchen." She went back upstairs and I didn't say anything.

At that moment, I knew something was wrong. My heart began to pound. "Wait here," I told Frank. I was scared as I slowly walked to the kitchen. Then I started breathing very hard.

I saw her head first then walked up to her and looked into her opened eyes. She wasn't moving or breathing. She looked as if she was telling me, "Nita, I couldn't fight any more, so I just laid down and died."

I started screaming and couldn't stop. I could feel Frank shaking me and lifting me from the floor. He carried me like a baby from the kitchen to the dining room. I could hear Sharon telling Dad to come home quick. "We can't wake up Mommy!" I was still screaming until I couldn't breathe anymore, then I felt Frank slapping me. When I was coming to, I remember hearing the nurse saying to give me a shot of something because I was going into shock, but I didn't want to think anymore, because I kept seeing her on the floor.

When I returned home from the hospital, people were already pouring into the house. People loved her. She listened to their problems and always tried to help out in some way, no matter how tired she was. She always let us have our friends over as long as we did our chores. She sacrificed everything so that she could make us happy. She would also cook for us because we never learned how, but did I ever say "thank you"? My sister and I would argue over who was going to do the dishes when instead we should have been grateful that we even had dirty dishes because we had eaten a meal. We could have done so much more to help her.

I kept trying to think of when I said, "I love you, thank you, Mommy." Did I ever tell her? I remember her telling me, but did I say it back? If I had to think that hard, then I must not have. I kept trying to find somewhere in the house where I could be alone so that I could weep for my mother, let out my sorrow for never telling her that I loved her or "thank you, Mommy for loving me." I'd give her cards on Mother's Day, but I never said it from my own lips. I looked in her bedroom and saw the few clothes she had that she'd never wear again. I looked at her shoes and imagined her weary legs and tired feet in them. I fell to my knees and wailed like the rain that fell that night. Family started pouring in.

The next day, Nadine and Debbie were there. Everybody kept crying and talking about the good days. Nadine kept calling her name, "Aunt Bet!'" That's what they called her. I snapped. "Shut up!" I screamed. I felt bad afterwards and told her I was sorry. This would be the second time I ever saw my daddy cry. The first time was when his mother died. He wasn't always good to my mother and neither were we, but it was too late to say we were sorry. We all took her for granted except for my brother, who loved her dearly. He took my father by the hands and held them tight. It was still raining. I looked out the window at the people walking and laughing in the rain and felt like I was the only one grieving for my mother. I became angry because I felt that all of those happy faces should be crying, too. I was tripping. It was weird. I would be awakened by the sound of her curling iron clicking in my sleep and then the smell coming from freshly curled hair. I was imagining and hearing things.

The day of the funeral seemed like it would never come, but I didn't want it to.

We were up early. The black hearse and cars were already outside. We walked out the door, first my dad and then my brother, followed by Sharon, myself, Emma, Debbie, and Nadine. We wore afros and purple and white dresses that came just above our knees. I was feeling sick to my stomach. We gave Mom the traditional last ride through the neighborhood before we parked in front of the church where I was baptized. Then got out of the cars and lined up. The church was so full inside that no one else could fit in so they formed lines outside on both sides of the church steps that lead down to Collom Street. I didn't want to go inside, but I missed my mom. All I wanted to do was to see her just one more time, but when I got inside the church, I was afraid to look up. I didn't want her to be dead. I held my head down as I walked to sit down.

The preacher began to give the eulogy. The only thing I remember him saying was that "She was always giving of herself. Always doing something for someone else, even when she was tired and sick. That's the kind of person she was." At that point I stood up, and that's when I heard him say, "That's right, child, go on and see your mother. Touch her. Don't be afraid."

I walked cautiously toward the coffin and looked into her face. She looked like she was smiling, but I really couldn't tell. I didn't look at her hands because I would have wept. Her hands would have reminded me of her hard life. I bent over to kiss her. She was cold. I thought that she would still be warm like she always was. Then I sat down. Sharon and Emma stood up, walked over to her coffin and bent over to kiss her, then Nadine and then Debbie.

After the funeral we walked through the double red doors of the church that led you back outside. There were so many people, and someone must have informed our former comrades from the Panther Party that our mom had passed away because as we walked down the church steps, a group of Panthers whose faces we had never seen before were there dressed in uniform to salute my mother by extending their arms forward with tightly clenched fists as the pall bearers carried her body back to the hearse.

Then something very strange happened. A dark shadow rolled like a boulder, starting from the church until it reached the other end of the street. After the darkness passed, then it rolled back up like a scroll until there was nothing but brightness again. Someone in the crowd said that God had walked by, and at that moment, I felt consoled.

I don't remember too much of the burial except that it started to rain again. I didn't want to see them lower her in the ground so I walked away. Ms. Robin told us that the worst part wasn't the funeral or the burial, but after everybody goes back home. You're left to start all over again without her. She was right. We didn't know our daddy.

My dad was a tall man, dark brown in color. He wasn't covered in hair, so his skin was smooth. The thing I feared about him the most was his temper. My dad was a proud man, someone who wouldn't accept charity. He didn't trust people either, especially the white race. When I had matured, he told me that his daddy was a gravedigger. One day they brought the body of a mutilated black man to a grave site to be buried. He said that the man had been very badly beaten and that his ears and private parts were missing. My dad was a man of very few words, even though he talked a little more when he was drinking, which was also when he would sing songs by the Mills Brothers and Ray Charles.

We saw more of his presence in the house when we were very young and less of him right before we entered our teenage years. We didn't know where he went on the weekends, so before we went to bed, we'd holler down to my mom and say "Goodnight, Mom" and then we'd lower our voices and say, "Goodnight, Dad, wherever you are." When we were very little, he would fight and argue with my mom and then he would get out his banjo and play a song called "Till Then." He taught Sharon the words and the melody to the song, and when she would sing it, he would cry, so she never liked to sing it. She asked him one day why that song made him cry? He said, "Because one day you will have your own mountains to climb."

For years I believed that my daddy loved my sister and not me because they were the same complexion, but then he called me into the kitchen soon after my mother's death and said that because I seemed to be the more responsible one between the two of us, he would teach me how to pay the bills and have my name added to his checks. He even called Big Jan over to the house and they both taught me how to prepare soul food.

There was a knock at the door.

"Who is it?" I asked.

"Mike," he said. "Can I speak to you for a couple of minutes?"

I peeked through the shades to see who was at my door because I had known several Mikes from the neighborhood.

"We're canvassing the area trying to get—Just a minute," I interrupted.

I opened the door. It was Mike from Summersville. I'd known him for a long time. *But what is he doing canvassing the neighborhood I live in?* I thought.

"We're canvassing the area in hopes of trying to get enough people interested in unifying the community and making it a more productive and safer environment for our families," he continued to say.

"Look around at your neighborhood. Drug dealers have taken over and now nowhere is safe. We still have white businessmen who work right here in our community and never give anything back. Not even a job to a black man. They just keep taking from us. Take a look at the Keystone directly across the street from where you live. Who owns it?" he asked.

"I think white people," I said.

"You're right," he said. "Now did you ever see a black man in that building working?" he asked.

I began to think to myself. "No," I said. That building was located in a black neighborhood and yet no black men were ever employed. He got me to thinking—he was right.

"We're having a meeting at the WAC building. Can you make it?" he asked.

"Yeah," I said. "I'll be there."

"Bring someone with you," he said.

"Okay," I responded.

And then I again wondered why he was down in my neighborhood trying to change things when Summerville had their own struggles, but he let me know that this was a coalition of communities working together for the same cause.

He said that they had already started a program in Summerville so he and a group of brothers came to Brickyard to get the ball rolling down here. The meeting was on a Wednesday evening at the WAC building just up the street and around the corner.

The turnout was good that evening. Mike introduced us to several other people working with him, Boom, Tick, and Emory. They called themselves the Group so we'd know who the group leaders would be.

That night, we addressed many of our concerns. At the next meeting we would be appointing a new block captain and a clean-up committee. We were looking forward to it because it had been so long since we had a clean-up. Mike encouraged us to invite more young people to the next meeting while he would try and get more adult participation.

We met again that next Wednesday, and the response was even better so we had an even larger turnout.

Ms. Turner was appointed our new block captain. She was a parent we all felt showed a willingness to work with the community. She was also a woman who was well respected by everyone in the community. Sharon, Emma, Patricia, Tick, Anita, Emory, Boom, and myself were all on the clean-up committee. We contacted the city and told them what we wanted to do, so we were given paint and brushes to paint our curbs and street addresses. They also gave us large trash bags and lent us their push brooms to clean the streets. We had collected money three days before the clean-up and had raised enough money to buy enough refreshments for everyone.

Several meetings would follow, and we seemed to be gaining the support we needed from the community. The block clean-up had been a success, so we decided to have at least one once a month.

Mike and Boom were former gang members from the same gang in Summerville. Tick was from Haines Street and Emory was from the Brickyard. They decided to organize a youth alliance, which would be known as the Youth Council.

It was important to the Group that they form a bond with the youth if they wanted to accomplish their goals. Besides, the drug dealers had already befriended a lot of the youth, so they needed positive male role models, especially since most families in the Brickyard were headed by two parents, but a lot of the fathers drank or were alcoholics.

We had churches on just about every corner, but so were bars or "beer gardens" as they were called then.

The neighborhood was changing fast and the church wasn't answering the needs of the growing problems. It had become a place of stagnation and complacency. The preacher would preach about what was going on and how all of this was prophesied in the Bible, but that's where it stopped. They weren't giving back anything to the community either. To me, church had lost its meaning.

A meeting would consist of a social gathering where we would just talk and play records. We didn't have any recreational facilities so activities were very limited. As time went by and because we were former Panthers and had an inside knowledge of the struggle and the task before us, Sharon, Emma, Anita, and myself met on a more regular basis, usually about three times a week. We would also include Patricia, even though she wasn't a former Panther, but she was always attentive at the meetings and always interested in what we had to say. The rest of the youth (mostly the Corner Boys) were excluded from these meetings because the group felt that they weren't ready to grasp the full gist of all that the struggle entailed. They had already started smoking reefer and some of them were probably into other drugs by now. I still remember the day they entered the home of the biggest drug dealer in our neighborhood. They were never the same; neither was home.

After our meetings, we would take turns and cook and then wash the dishes. Whenever a meeting was called, we were there. Our motto was, "Be ready when called."

Then the youth alliance tried something new. At one of the meetings we wanted any young person who was serious about ridding the community of drugs to come forward. Some came forward with anticipation while some came reluctantly and some not at all. The next meeting would be half of what we had before and the next one even less. Like I mentioned before, the drug dealers had already befriended a lot of the youth.

More time would go by. Drug dealers were now openly doing their business on the corners, in the alleys by the Keystone, in the daytime, at nighttime—it didn't matter to them where or when they sold their drugs.

At our next meeting, we declared an all-out war on drug activity. This divided those of us who wanted to rid the community of drugs from those who didn't. Mike said that we were a positive force while those who wanted to continue to degenerate were a negative element. The Corner Boys didn't accept what Mike had to say because they liked getting high, even though they liked socializing when we would come together for the meetings, but the term *negative element* was offensive to them. They knew that Mike was referring to the rest of the Corner Boys who refused to ever attend any of the meetings so at the next meeting they came with an attitude and left with one, never to return. The only ones to remain were the Group, which had by now increased in membership, and those of us who were chosen to meet on a more regular basis. Donald and Renee were the youngest members of the council, and they decided to stay also.

Then things started to get ugly when the drug dealers accepted the term *negative element* and would scoff at us whenever they saw us gathered together in a group. Eventually anyone in the community who approved of drug activity or who defended drug dealers would also accept the term *negative element*, so we adopted another slogan: "You're either a part of the problem or a part of the solution."

We were now known as the Pos, (short for *positive element*), while the drug dealers and users were known as the Negs (short for *negative element*). We got word that death threats were made on Mike's and Emory's lives. Then we were told that the Negs would be dealt with for making the threat, and that night, two Negs were shot. You never saw one of us without the other after that.

The group decided to close down a drug house that was doing big business on Wakefield Street. We knew that this was where a lot of the young people got their dope from. We would need the community behind us because the cops had all but abandoned us a long time ago. There was a meeting planned on how the group would confront Diamond, the biggest drug dealer in the area.

The group decided to walk up to his door and let him know that we were aware of his drug activities. He refused to cease selling drugs from his house and by the next week his home had burned down to the ground. But he wasn't the only one selling drugs.

The group continued to stress the importance of continuing the block clean-ups as a means of instilling dignity in ourselves and taking pride in our communities again. That would mean no more graffiti on the walls and no more whiskey bottles and trash along the streets and in the alleys.

Volunteers would have to keep the grass cut in areas where a house or storefront once stood and had now become a haven for rats and an empty lot for weeds to grow.

Our meetings became more political. We were often told that the Panthers were ahead of their time, and that they had moved too fast. They started on Z and should have started on A.

The Group theorized that in order for us to move forward and develop, we would have to start with our politicians, which made a lot of sense because they had the power to make decisions and the people had the power to dictate what those decisions would be based on the needs of the community and then enforce those decisions. But first we had to get an apathetic community to come out to register and vote. We canvassed from door to door urging people to vote only for politicians who would meet the needs of their constituents.

During that time, black people were brainwashed into believing that the Democrats were the only politicians who served the needs of the black and poor communities and that the Republicans catered to the rich white people. Nobody ever talked about the Independent politicians. We were taught to vote only one way, and that was STRAIGHT DEMOCRATIC! But not anymore. Whoever was going to get the job done and answer the needs of the people would get our vote.

Our first test came when we heard of a man who wanted to run for state representative. We studied his agenda and felt that he would be someone we would support even though he ran on an Independent ticket. His name was David P. Richardson.

We did all the leg and footwork and urged the community to study his agenda before making a decision. Dave won the election, and then came more meetings, our reward for a job well done.

My social life had changed drastically. I hardly spent any time with Frank, although he wanted me to, but there was always a meeting.

He told me one day, "You think of your organization more than you do me.

They come first in your life."

"Then come to the meetings," I said. "I always invite you, but you never come. You know how it was when we were Panthers. I'm just continuing the work. That's all. I thought you'd always feel the same way, even after you left the Panther Party. You said that you would always be a part of the struggle. I don't want for us to break up. That's why I want you to come to one of the meetings. That way you can see what we are all about and we can see each other more."

He shook his head and sighed.

I began to yell. "I know what it is!" I said. "You're from Preppy Mount Airy. You're getting comfortable up there in your nice neighborhood. You've forgotten about the struggle!"

"What are you talking about girl?" he yelled back. "I still believe in the struggle.

It's just that I came out of the service and went right into the Panther Party. I never gave myself a chance to clear my head after all that fuckin' war. I'm twenty-one and look at me. I'm still living with my mom. I need time to do something for me. And I want to do something for us." He paused for a moment. "Look," he said. "Don't ever think that because I live in Mount Airy that I think that I'm better. I'm black. I'll always be a black man. Where I live don't change that fact." He paused again and then bit down on his lip. "When's the next meeting?"

"I'll call you," I said.

Before we went to bed, Sharon and I had a conversation about our relationships.

"What are you gonna do about you and Tony?" I asked. "He's never gonna join us," I said frankly.

"I don't know," she said. "We're drifting so far apart. I feel like we're just one more meeting away from calling it quits."

"Frank said he's coming to the next meeting."

"You're lucky," she said. "At least Frank listens when you talk about the struggle. He was there. He knows the deal. Tony was never into the struggle like that. All he did was grow an afro."

"I'll tell Frank to talk to him. He respects Frank," I said.

Mike had a thing for Patricia. I could tell by the way he looked at her all the time, the way he played around with her. She liked him too. She just wasn't admitting it.

He started asking me questions about her that showed me just how interested he was! If they got together, I thought they'd make a good couple. Eventually, she had become his girl. She was also the first of us to lose her virginity.

One night she said that she was going to his house, but the next morning her cousin came knocking on our door looking for her. I knew then that she had spent the night with Mike.

We stayed on the porch for awhile and not too long after that, Patricia came walking down the street. We ran to meet her. She was grinning, or "cheesin'," as we called it.

"You did it!" I said. "Ooh, you did it. You got laid, didn't you?"

I was curious. I had to know what it was like.

"Tell me, what it was like, Patricia?" I asked.

"Yeah, tell us," Sharon asked.

She started cheesin' again.

"Well," she said. "It hurt at first, but then it felt good."

We all started to giggle, and then later on that day, we were called to another meeting.

Frank finally came to a meeting. Since he was a former Panther, he was received whole heartedly by the group. He shared his experiences with everybody as a Panther. He seemed to like the meetings and came to several more. Then one day he stopped coming altogether.

"Why did you stop coming to the meetings?" I asked.

"I don't like them," he said.

"Why?" I asked.

"Because something about them ain't right."

"What do you mean?"

"Well it's something about them that's too controlling," he said. "I mean, every time you turn around, they're having a meeting and you have to be there. What if I have to be somewhere else that's just as important? It don't mean anything to them. The organization comes first. Forget everything else. We'll just have to see each other whenever you don't have a meeting," he said sarcastically. But I'm out. I don't want a part of them. I don't need them telling me where I have to be and what time to be there."

So that was the decision Frank made. The group increased in my life, and he decreased.

At our next meeting I informed the group that he would not be coming back.

"Everyone wasn't called for this work," Tick said. "As much as you want to be with Frank, you can't. The struggle comes first." He was right. Frank had become history.

Tension began to build between the Group and the community. We were the Pos's and they were the Neg's. I had gotten a job and had to quit after one week because it wasn't safe for us to walk the streets alone anymore. It got to the point where we were told that if there was anywhere we had to go or anything we had to do, to make sure that there was a need to do it. It was important that it be something necessary, or else abstain from it. That would mean no more going to the movies."

Lady Sings the Blues came out that year and I wanted to see it real bad, but I knew that the group would say, "no!"

But then they made plans for all of us who wanted to go to meet at Boom's house. I was surprised but glad to be going somewhere else besides a meeting. Later on that night I questioned Sharon as to why all of a sudden the group had a need to see *Lady Sings the Blues*.

"Mike said that it had to be related to the struggle," I said. They weren't talking about any struggle in that movie. I knew what it was—they wanted to see the movie like everybody else, but if I wanted to see something, then I couldn't go.

Sharon was changing. She justified everything they did and said. "Well, Mike said it did relate to the struggle," she said. "We discussed it at a meeting before they said we could go."

I chuckled, but I was pissed. "Tell me," I said, how does *Lady Sings the Blues* relate to the struggle?"

"Well," she said, "remember how the white man took advantage of Diana Ross and Richard Pryor by getting them hooked on drugs?"

"Yeah," I said.

"Well, that's for real. It's happening right here in our neighborhood." Everything she said made sense and was just another shot in the arm for me to go to another meeting.

The Group had now changed their name to the core. Core members took turns patrolling the streets making sure that no drug activity was going on. Things started to look a lot better, like when I was growing up.

I looked up at the corner and thought about how bad things used to be before Mike came to our neighborhood. The Negs used to remind me of roaches, but today they are almost nowhere to be found. It was as though someone had sprayed a can of human insecticide and they were beginning to disappear.

They feared us, but we had to make them fear us because they didn't have any respect for anybody. Not your mother, your father, your sister, your brother, your grandparents, your children—NOBODY!

Then Emma got pregnant.

I was glad that I was going to be an aunt, but the group didn't believe in having babies. They said that there was no place for babies in the struggle; that there wasn't anytime to raise a baby. "We have too much work to do," they would say.

Too much yet to accomplish. Yeah, there was a time for sexual needs to be fulfilled, just don't get pregnant.

She was instructed to get an abortion, but inside she had already made a decision not to have it done.

Eight months later, she gave birth to a baby girl.

The brothers were always complaining that she was missing too many meetings. We were called to another meeting and Emma was told that she had to be there. She was breastfeeding and again was instructed to give the baby a bottle instead, since the brothers felt that bottle feeding would keep her from missing future meetings. This was a stressful time for her because they would never understand the bond between a mother and her baby.

She was angry and so was I. We discussed it with Sharon and Patricia, but they were a part of the core. They agreed with the brothers.

"It is something that we have to come to accept," they said. "That's what the struggle is about—sacrificing to achieve our goals, giving up what we want to do. There is no need to breastfeed," they said. "Next time, don't get pregnant."

Another meeting was called to discuss birth-control.

Birth control was something that wasn't talked about when I was growing up. People in my neighborhood had large families and if your mom had about twelve or thirteen kids, then the way we saw it, was that your parents liked doing it all the time. Neither sex nor birth control were discussed in school.

I once asked some woman how you stopped having babies, and she said, "you don't." You're only going to get as many as God gives you." It wasn't until girls were popping up pregnant at an alarming rate that sex education was incorporated into the school curriculum.

Emma stopped breastfeeding.

I resented the core for making her go against what she really wanted to do, and that was breastfeed her baby, but that didn't change my mind about wanting to be a part of the core.

The core was the central part of the group; the entire backbone. That's why they changed their name, to give more meaning to who they were. They would be ready to give up everything for the struggle, even their lives, and at any given moment. They represented everything that we stood for and I wanted IN!

There was something about them that linked them closer together. At times when I was around them, I felt like an outcast, almost like they were the untouchables. Yeah, we all started out on A, but I felt now like they were somewhere on W and I was still stuck on A in my development as a revolutionist.

But then I also knew in my heart that some things I would never stop believing. At times I felt that you had to give up your mind, your thoughts, and your opinions to be a part of them, like when I was told to denounce God. I didn't want to. To me that would be committing spiritual suicide. They believed that any religious ideas that you continued to latch onto stunted your growth as a revolutionist. Their theory was if you believed that God was going to do everything, then you wouldn't do anything. And Frank once told me, "If there is a God, then He might as well take up a gun and help us fight."

So I eventually kept my opinions to myself, but Sharon would soon say that my attitude about Emma's situation was one of the reasons why I couldn't be a part of the core. "You're still too soft," she said. "You can't let stuff like that bother you."

Another reason why I couldn't get in was because I wouldn't denounce God.

Then one day the core scheduled a meeting at a member's house, and I got their first, followed by Tick, so now we were the only two there. He came on to me for sex. I was shocked.

"You got a girl," I said.

"Who?" he said. Tick had a stuttering problem whenever he got nervous or excited.

"Reah," I said. "Besides, I belong to Frank."

"I-I-I don't like Reah cau-cau-cau she uh-uh-uhgly.

"You are wrong!" I lashed out. "Plus you are gonna get dealt with for trying to take liberties with me."

"Uh-uh-ugly Reah," he said, "That's what I call her. They won't believe you anyway. Go on and tell. I-I-I don't care. N-N-Now give me some."

I remained steadfast.

Then there was a knock at the door. It was Sharon, Patricia, and Mike. I pulled Sharon to the side and told her what Tick tried to do. She became furious and relayed it to the rest of the core. He was confronted immediately, but denied the whole thing. Sharon came back and told me what the outcome was.

"He denied it," she said, "and we have to take his word over yours."

I was crushed and I started to cry. When we got home, she expressed to me that she believed me.

"They all believed you," she said. "We could tell that he was straight up lying, but that's the way it is. We have to take his word over yours. Our commitment to him is stronger than our commitment to you."

I no longer wanted to be a part of the core or have any part of them. Then Emma dropped out. I was freaking out. I wanted to leave too, but I was too afraid. If I left, then I wouldn't have any more protection. I was held in thrall by a group who had become my lifeline.

After that, Emma stayed at home taking care of her baby and then she eventually moved in with her boyfriend. I envied her because she didn't have anymore meetings to go to, and even though she had a baby to care for, at least she had her life back.

A couple of weeks went by. Sharon had just returned home from a Core meeting.

"You're in," she said. They had made me a member of the core, but at this stage of my life, I didn't know if that was good or bad.

I went to my very first meeting and was told that I couldn't tell anybody about anything we discussed. And then more meetings. And then classes. We learned martial arts and then I was handed a gun. I was taught how to clean it, how to take it apart and put it back together, and how to load it, aim it, and shoot it. I was fast and I had aim.

At one meeting I attended, we watched The Battle of Algiers and were given The Red Book, which was the teachings of Mao Tse Tung. My spirit had been renewed. *The Red Book* was now my Bible.

If I had any reservations or questions about joining the core, they were answered. I was a communist, a revolutionist, ready to give my life for the struggle.

Time went by. It got to the point where my sister and I weren't safe in our home anymore. Members of the core took turns sleeping by the living room window with shotguns so that we could get some sleep. I feared for my father's life. He worked at night and would walk up the street to where his place of work was, Monday through Friday. I kept thinking that they would shoot him one of these times when he opened the door just to get there revenge, but the core said that our house had to be used as a stakeout. We were at war with the Negs.

Marvin Gaye had a song out that summer titled "What's Going On? " I began to wonder. Things were getting out of control, just crazy.

Then someone informed my dad that these guys would come in his house when he left for work. He asked us if it was true, and of course we said "no."

He didn't believe us and told us to keep those motherfuckers out of his goddamn house. So now we had more people to fear, my dad and the Negs.

We had a meeting the next day to discuss what we needed to do because my dad didn't want anyone in his house. By this time a contract was out on my sister because word had gotten back to the Negs that she carried a piece up under her turban and when the opportunity presented itself, she was to be shot on the spot. That freaked me out. That was my sister, whom I loved dearly. I was scared for her.

The core had concluded that if my dad didn't comply with their needs, then he had to be dealt with, too. Sharon still had this commitment thing to the core.

"I want out," I said. "They're talking 'bout dealing with Dad. What do they mean?" I yelled. "What do they think they are going to do to him?" I asked.

"I don't know," she said, "But dad is a Neg."

"He ain't no Neg!" I yelled.

"Yeah, but he don't care about the struggle. Even your parents can be negative elements."

"Y'all are all crazy," I said. "They got you brainwashed." I left her presence.

I had become depressed again. I couldn't take another meeting.

Then things turned for the worst.

We were called to an emergency meeting that was being held at the WAC building. Something serious was going to take place. The core hadn't informed the Council members because they didn't want to cause any fear. I wasn't even supposed to know, but I found out through Sharon. I had a bad feeling that day, like somebody was going to die. Maybe it would be me, or my sister. I didn't want to die at the hands of a drug dealer or at the hands of an addict, but I didn't want to lay down my life for the core either. I would have died twice. I had already died once, and that was when they took my freedom from me, but I was a member of the core. I had to be there. "Be ready when called." I was trying to find out why this emergency meeting was being called at the WAC building. What was going on?

The phone rang. It was time to go. We emerged from our houses. The core, who represented the Pos, were in full force outside my door. We were strong in number that day. I looked all around me. The Negs were now all gathered together on the corner like roaches again, something they hadn't done in awhile.

We walked up the street toward the WAC building. Once we got there, females were instructed to sit in the back while all the males had to sit in the front. I felt like I was being used as a sitting duck. I was nervous and I couldn't shake this feeling I had. I felt like I was in the trenches in Vietnam ready to be attacked by the enemy at any moment. I could tell that Mike was trying to keep his cool, but I could read his eyes, his body language. He was nervous and anxious. He kept trying to give us the impression that everything was cool, and that this was just another meeting, but I kept getting this other message from his body language.

I looked around at the other council members. They weren't feeling what I was feeling. They weren't informed that something serious was going to take place. They were laughing and talking with one another. I kept looking toward the back door to see how far away we were from it in case we had to get out. At that moment it looked very far away. *Would we all make it out in time?* I thought. I kept moving around in my seat, nervous and uneasy. Mike was talking, but I was tuned out to what he was saying.

I kept looking back at the door. Then there was a knock. I knew that once they unlocked that door, all hell was going to break loose, and it did. I saw the Negs enter the building. Fighting broke out and then the sound of gunshots came from everywhere. We made it to the back door, but when we opened it, there were more rooms and doors. None of us were familiar with our surroundings because we had never been in that area of the WAC building before, only core members. It wasn't until the first core member made it out that we were able to get to the outside of the building.

Once outside, we ended up in a large yard surrounded by a concrete wall. Little Jase was an addict. He hated us with a passion, especially my sister. He used to say that he would be the one to put a cap in her head. We weren't safe, and we knew we had to get out fast.

Then all of a sudden I looked up and saw Little Jase walking across the concrete wall with a gun in his hand. He was about five feet nine inches with a stocky build. His eyes were red and dazed. He looked like he was walking in slow motion. His right arm moved with the motion of his body as he continued to walk a straight line down the concrete wall. He had a very angry and deranged look on his face. His eyes began to race at the crowd of panicking Council and Core members below him. I felt helpless. I had learned how to use a gun, but I was without protection. I kept following his eyes, and then I looked toward my sister. He fixed his eyes upon hers and started shooting.

I was waiting for her to drop at any minute, but she kept running. I looked up at him again. He was re-loading his gun while everybody was trying to get over the wall. Sharon had made it. He continued to look for her, but she was gone, then I saw his eyes racing again. This time he was staring at me. He pointed the gun at me. I started to run and he started shooting. I kept looking back at him. He wouldn't stop shooting his gun. I was waiting to feel a bullet hit me in the back.

It was living a nightmare. I ran toward the wall and tried to climb it, but it was too high. No one was there to push me over. I felt weak. I looked over again at Little Jase, who was re-loading his gun again. If I was going to live, then I had to make it over that wall. I ran away from the wall, then ran toward it again with all my might, scaling it with my feet and hands until I could feel the top. I kept pulling myself up until someone from the other side touched my hand and began to pull me over. Once my body was on top of the wall, I jumped to the ground. No one was there. I don't know who helped me over the wall. I ran until I found my sister, then we ran to the home of an Italian family who owned a bread shop in our community. We banged on her door.

"Help us," we pleaded. "Someone is going to shoot us. "We were breathing hard and sweating.

I didn't think that she would let us in her house, but she did. We kept thanking her. We could hear the sounds of sirens everywhere.

"There's a large doghouse in the backyard. Hide in it until you think it's safe to come out," she said.

We crawled in it. She had a picket fence that surrounded her yard. We never made a sound. Then we saw Little Jase through the spaces in the picket fence walking by with the gun still in his hand. He had the same deranged and evil expression on his face as he continued to walk in a slow motion-like manner.

We continued to stay motionless and as far back in the doghouse as we could get.

We remained inside until it was pitch black outside, then carefully emerged from the doghouse feeling cramped and scared. We slowly unlocked the gate and when we thought it was safe to leave, we ran through the back alleys until we ended up in our backyard.

The next day, everybody was talking about the shoot-out. My dad heard about it, but never knew we were in it. I wondered if anybody from the Council or the Core was killed. Then the telephone rang, and we were told that nobody from our side was shot, but several Negs were. Some had life-threatening wounds.

I left the group after that, but my sister remained. She just couldn't break free. They still had her mind. I was angry at her. She didn't want me to leave.

"I'm out," I said angrily.

"What about your protection?" she asked.

"I don't care," I said. "If they're going to get me then they're just going to have to get me. Why are you stayin'? We can't win. We lost." By this time I had become very emotional. "Just look outside," I said. "They're everywhere, just like roaches. The Negs won!" I screamed angrily.

Every day we began to pull at each other. She tried to get me to come back, and I kept trying to get her to leave.

I wouldn't go out of the house for anything. I knew I didn't have any more protection. We were running low on food. The Core wasn't around because everybody was still laying low.

Then about two weeks later, Sharon told me that she was leaving the Core. It was the best news I had heard in a long time.

It was on a Sunday. Emma was all dressed up. "Where are you going?" I asked.

"Church," she said. "I'm going back to church."

"I'll go with you next Sunday," I said.

I went upstairs and looked in my mom and dad's bedroom. Mom's shoes were still placed neatly under her dresser, just the way she left them.

They say that paradise is at the feet of your mother. I knelt down at her shoes and kissed them. At that moment, I was in paradise.

"Be good to your mother, take care of her. She's good to you," just like Joe used to tell me. "Listen to her," he would say. I love you, Joe. I wished that I could have kissed her feet, but that was now impossible. Kiss your mother's feet while there is breath still in her body.

I realized that I couldn't be a prisoner in my own neighborhood if I was going to live in it. God had always been my protection, not the Core. Besides, I was hungry.

"I'm hungry," I said to Sharon. "Walk with me to the store."

We stood on the porch and looked up the street. The Negs were already gathered together. We were scared, but we wanted something to eat so we decided to go anyway. We thought they were going to start capping. At one time they were our homeboys, or the Corner Boys, as we called them. They continued to stare and we stared back. None of us were smiling. My eyes began to fill with tears. Then all of a sudden they turned and walked away. They went their way and we went ours.

At that moment I questioned myself, *Was the struggle over? Or was the revolution just a blueprint of our imagination?*

I began to ponder the thought as we entered the store. Hell, no! I concluded. For even now where negative elements are gathered together, there will the struggle find itself.

Power to the Pos!